THE OTHER
MOSS

To Tammy Allen
with best wishes
A. C. Moss

May 2011

Happiness is racing a three-wheel Morgan!

THE OTHER MOSS

E. Alan Moss

Reminiscences of a Life
With Cars and Horses

Foreword by Peter Egan

Sir Stirling Moss was arguably the finest racing car driver
of the last century. As we shared the last name, I was
frequently asked if I was Stirling or if we were related.

At the Monterey Historic races, Sir Stirling
asked me for my autograph! *

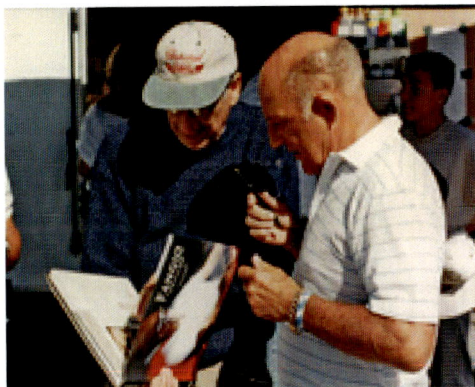

*Just kidding – I am getting <u>his</u> autograph!

This book was written and composed using the latest and most sophisticated electronic equipment available.

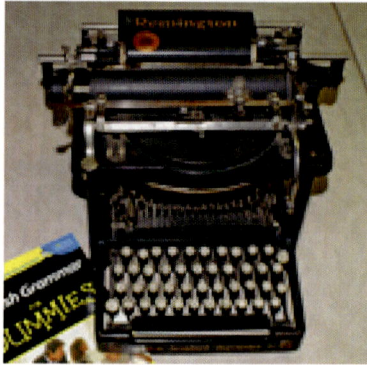

The type style is Baskerville.

First Edition
Second Printing

E. Alan Moss
Sedona, Arizona
www.racermoss.com

Printed in the United States of America by Instantpublisher

ISBN: 978-1-60458-221-5

FOREWORD

MY FRIEND, THE OTHER MOSS

Sitting here at the word processor in my Wisconsin home office, I have only to swivel my chair toward the bookshelves on my left to see the words "Moss Motors" emblazoned on a whole row of catalogs for car parts. They're filed right in the middle of a large (too large, any sane person might say) wall of books on British cars – MG, Jaguar, Austin-Healey, Triumph, Morgan, Lotus and so on. Inspect those catalogs closely, and you'll find them well-thumbed, stained with genuine greasy fingerprints and reeking faintly of hypoid gear oil from one of the three MGs I've restored. Or maybe from one of the Sprites or TR-3s, or the '67 E-type.

You see, like the author of this book, I fell in love with cars – and British cars in particular – at an early age, falling victim to the charms of the MG TC on first sight, as if knocked off my horse by a lightning bolt. This neurological damage led to an early career as a foreign car mechanic and a lifetime of restoring and racing old British sports cars. Parts were needed, of course, and I soon found myself sending off for Moss Motors catalogs and mailing large sums of money to someplace called Goleta, California.

But not until 7 or 8 years ago did I finally meet E. Alan Moss, the founder of this famous company, who had long since retired and moved to Sedona, Arizona. I had friends who were vintage car racers in Sedona, and they kept saying, "You've just got to meet Al Moss. He's a great guy – a real spark plug of the sports car scene here – and he lives right over there."

I finally met Al, and they were right. He is a great guy, a real spark plug of the sports car scene, and he did indeed live right over there. In a lovely high desert home with a view of Sedona's famous red buttes and a nice garage filled with, among other things, a Morgan 4/4, a Triumph 650 Tiger and his original MG TC. All of which he works on and maintains himself.

To be around Al Moss for any length of time is to suspect that someone has slipped Prozac into your morning orange juice while Al, meanwhile, has been busily downing six cups of coffee. He's energetic, funny, highly intelligent and filled with new ideas, as well as clear and vivid memories of the past. And what a past.

Al was one of the founders of the sports car movement in California just after WWII. He raced, ran a repair shop, officiated at all the now-legendary races on the West Coast, founded a badly-needed MG parts business and hung out with a colorful cast of racers, pioneer tuners and car builders whose like we probably won't see again. All in a magical era when sports cars were not just machines but a way of life, a way of looking at the world.

He's also a fine photographer, writer and raconteur, so his friends have been leaning on him for years to "write all this stuff down." Well, he finally did. And here it is, presented with enthusiasm, heart and a sparkling sense of good fun.

Al doesn't know how to do it any other way.

Peter Egan
January, 2008

PREFACE

For the past few years several friends and acquaintances have suggested that I write a book about my life. While I could not imagine more than a dozen people actually buying a book about Al Moss, I decided to give it a go and see what happens.

Actually, I *have* had a full and interesting life and, most importantly, it has been extremely enjoyable.

I wish to begin with an apology. I am well aware that critics may, and probably will, find fault with my style of writing. I have no pretensions of being a writer, but have done my best to portray many aspects of a long and happy life and career.

As it is impossible to compose this book in strict chronological sequence, I have put a timeline on the following page.

I am aware that some folks go through life looking for typographical and other mistakes; they should be well satisfied with this book.

In conclusion, let me say that I cannot properly express the gratitude I feel to those countless friends whom I have met on my journey through life, and to those who helped with the editing of this great tome.

And, finally, if you are not satisfied with your purchase of this book, please recycle it, rather than throwing it into the trash.

Al Moss
Sedona, Arizona

TIMELINE

1927   E. Alan enters the world in Cleveland Ohio.

1933   The Moss family migrates to California.

1946   Graduation from high school.

1947   Quit college to begin apprenticeship.

1948   Acquisition of MG TC sports car.

1949   Opened first auto repair shop.

1950   Opened car dealership.

1951   The Big Wreck.

1953   New shop built in Los Angeles.

1963   Moved Moss Motors & family to Santa Barbara.

1963   Equestrian activities begin.

1975   Entered first of many historic automobile races.

1976   de Anza Trek and Bicentennial Rally.

1977   Sold Moss Motors and retired.

1997   Moved from Santa Barbara to Sedona Arizona.

2007   Celebrated eightieth birthday in grand style.

2008   Published my first and last book. This epic!

2008   Writing a supplement to this book: *Moss's MG Memoirs*

CONTENTS

1 A Brief Family History

I was born in Cleveland, Ohio, on January 6th, 1927, and have been hanging around ever since. I started out as E. Alan Moss, the E standing for a very nice name, which shall remain a secret forever. (Actually, the E is for Emergency.)

Surviving the pangs of birth, my childhood began in a nice environment, which I enjoyed as an only child. With no sibling rivalry, I was thoroughly spoiled.

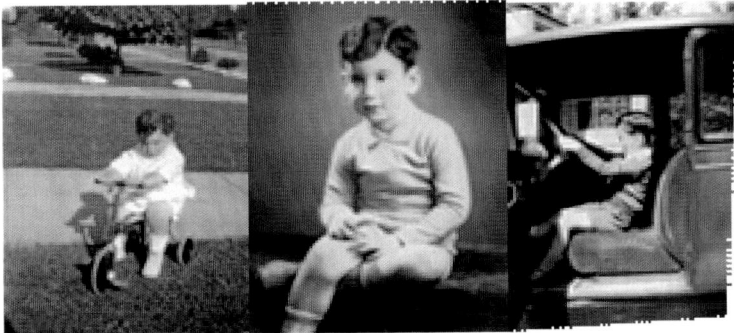

20 months   *Age 3*   *Age 5*

My parents must have been fairly well off financially; I remember a nice house, a maid and a Cadillac touring car. From early childhood, I suffered from both asthma and an avid interest in anything to do with automobiles.

Like many (too many) folks in the terrible depression, my parents lost nearly everything, and, like the Joads, we packed our few belongings into our 1927 Buick and headed for the land of opportunity and endless sunshine – California.

Dad & Buick at Boulder Dam. July, 1933

As my parents were forced to relocate many times, I attended a succession of different schools, finally settling into John Burroughs Junior High School in Los Angeles. I graduated from Los Angeles High School in 1946, and after a brief stint in college, began my career in the automotive trade.

In 1949, I married Joan Fetterman and we became the proud parents of two charming girls: Juli in 1953 and Cindy in 1956. The reason we had only two children was that we read somewhere that every third baby born into the world was Chinese, and we didn't feel able to cope with a foreign child.

Joan and I divorced in 1970, and the following year I married Nancy Brown. We divorced in 1985, and a year later I began a long-term relationship with Lynda McEvoy, and we are still, happily, together.

At this time of writing (2008), Joan and Nancy are alive and well, as are daughters Juli and Cindy, both of whom live in California. Juli has provided me with four grandchildren and two great-grandchildren.

That's enough personal stuff.

2   School Daze

My years in school were not particularly happy ones. I was not a very good student and was not terribly interested in learning "all that junk." As it happened, I had (have?) a fairly high IQ, and I heard many teachers say, "Alan has the ability if he would only apply himself." I did manage to squeeze through school and apparently a sufficient amount of the learning seeped into my wee brain – perhaps by osmosis? I subsequently learned that a good education is vitally important in order to survive in today's business and social world. Even today, working in my shop, I frequently put to use what I learned in algebra and geometry.

Fortunately, my junior high school had a comprehensive auto shop, which had three display chassis and three engines, donated by the manufacturers. Another fellow and I actually got one, an ancient Durant engine, running. It had no radiator, nor muffler, and, believe me, the entire school heard it run!

While I was in junior high school, I wanted nothing more than a car of my very own, not to drive but to dismantle and learn what makes a car tick. I yearned after a Model T Ford because Model Ts were pretty cheap. One day, on my way home from school, I saw a somewhat dilapidated, 1929 Model A Ford sedan, with a *For Sale* sign where the windshield used to be. A cowboy had driven it from Prescott, Arizona, to Los Angeles, only to have the engine freeze solid on Wilshire Boulevard.

After some serious haggling, I purchased the car for the grand sum of seven dollars. My father towed it home and the following Saturday, with help and advice from a few neighbors, and very few tools, I began dismantling the engine. I also had help from several library books, such as

Dyke's Automobile Encyclopedia. After a few skinned knuckles, and many band-aids, I found to my delight that the engine was not frozen, which would have been quite serious, but that a bolt had become wedged between the flywheel and its housing. Turning the crankshaft backward released the stuck bolt and, after a few days work I actually got the engine running – I was proud of my accomplishment.

Shortly after buying the Model A.   *Mom going for a test drive!*

I spent the entire summer working on this car, removing the sedan body and installing a roadster body I purchased for three dollars. I wanted to replace the original, large-diameter wire wheels with 16-inch disk wheels and tires. As this was wartime, it was impossible to purchase new tires, so I bought a complete, non-running, 1935 Pontiac convertible for ten dollars, towed it home and removed the tires. Early on a Saturday morning, a friend and I towed the car several miles to the nearest junkyard, leaving four white gouges in newly resurfaced Washington Boulevard, to the dismay of a policeman. Once there, I swapped the Pontiac for a set of 16-inch disk wheels to fit my Ford.

I now had the makings of a true hotrod. I painted the car bright red (what else?) and with white wheels and no fenders, it was the Cat's Meow.

I drove the Ford for a year or so and sold it in favor of a 1933 Chevrolet sedan – not a very trendy car, but something different to work on while learning all about the infamous "stovebolt" engine. This car was replaced by a 1937 Willys sedan.

1933 Chevy   *1937 Willys*

My next project was a 1938 Chevrolet coupe that had been totaled by a fire. I rebuilt this car, painted it black, and, immediately after the war was over, purchased a new set of tires and drove it to Iowa, with my mother, for a family wedding – an enjoyable trip with no car problems.

1938 Chevy, before…   …and after.

It was still impossible to purchase a new car; used cars were scarce and being sold at exorbitant prices. Therefore, I placed a sealed bid on a 1940 Dodge sedan that had been burned out in a fire. My high bid made me the proud owner of this hulk. I purchased the entire interior from a wrecked Chrysler Royal and managed to squeeze this luxurious interior: seats, dashboard and all, into the Dodge. After replacing all of the Dodge insignia with Chrysler logos, the car became known as the Crodge, or Dysler.

1940 Dodge

Now the Crodge

Upon selling the Crodge, I purchased a completely original 1931 Chevy roadster. I drove this car for a few years until I purchased a new, 1948 MG TC roadster. More about this car later.

My MG TC when brand new.

3 An MG and a Career Enter My Life

After struggling through twelve years of grade school, I graduated in 1946 and received a diploma, which certified that I was *smart*. I then enrolled in college, majoring in mechanical engineering, and, while struggling with some pretty serious courses, I began wondering what I would do if I succeeded in becoming a mechanical engineer. I really wanted to work with cars, not become a pencil pusher, but realized in order to succeed in the automotive trade, it would be necessary to specialize in a particular field. After some research, I made the decision to specialize in chassis and wheel alignment. The more I studied, the more aware I became that this would be an interesting and profitable field to pursue.

One of the top wheel alignment shops in Los Angeles was Bagge & Son. In addition to operating a clean, well-organized shop, they had designed a set of wheel-alignment instruments, which were superior to anything on the market at the time. I managed to worm my way into this shop as an apprentice, at the grand sum of twenty-five dollars a week!

After working at Bagge & Son for nearly a year, the owners felt I was competent enough for them to open a satellite shop and put me in charge. This was near downtown Los Angeles, and was scheduled to open in August of 1948. Prior to opening the new shop, a friend and I spent a week driving my 1931 Chevy roadster to Yosemite and San Francisco – a fun, trouble-free experience for two young fellas. Upon my return, I had a meeting with the man who was financing production of the wheel-alignment gauges, as well as the soon-to-be opened

shop. His office was located in Los Angeles on Figueroa Street, known as "Automobile Row," – with several miles of new car dealerships and used car lots.

All through this meeting, I was gazing across the street at a shiny little red roadster. I had been reading several British car magazines and I recognized this car as an MG TC. Immediately following the meeting, I crossed the street and spent a long time examining this beauty. I knew, then and there, that I *must* have one. There was just one thing standing in my way, or more precisely, several thousand things.

A new MG at that time was priced at something like $2,385, plus tax & license; well-used ones were available for slightly less. A few weeks later, I saw a TC advertised for sale in the *Los Angeles Times*.

The importer, Gough Industries, was also the distributor for Philco radios, refrigerators and TV sets. They ran a contest: 25 words or less on "Why I like a Philco TV." The first prize was a brand-spanking-new MG TC. A woman, married with two little children, won the car, had no use for it, and that was the ad I saw. I made arrangements to purchase the TC for $1750.

The night of September 13th, 1948, I showed up to pay for the car. There were two well-dressed men in the house – dealers it turned out. A bidding war ensued and I was sure I had lost the car. I bid $2050. They quit, and the sellers and I were ecstatic – they really wanted me to have the car. I had no idea how I was going to come up with a few hundred dollars more. But I did. Happily, I ended up with a brand new MG TC, red with a tan leather interior, exactly what I had wanted from the beginning. So, even though I have owned this car since new, I am not the original owner.

As was typical of many early MGs, neither the speedometer nor the tachometer was functioning. When I contacted the hardheaded Dutchman in charge of Gough Industries, he refused to replace the instruments, claiming that, as I was not the original owner, even though the car was brand new, he did not have to honor the warranty. So, I bit the bullet and purchased two new and very expensive instruments.

The previously mentioned shop that Bagge & Son opened for me was located in a big garage at 6th and Westmoreland in Los Angeles. The owner of the garage operated a fleet of pre-war Packard and Cadillac, chauffer-driven limousines, all black and kept spotless. I never tired of looking at these beauties.

I ran this shop for several months before the owners closed it, due of lack of business.

A Brief History of MG Distribution

William Morris (later to become Sir William Morris and then Lord Nuffield) built his first car in 1912 and, surprise, called it a *Morris*. In 1923, Cecil Kimber, a Morris employee, and later the manager, modified a Morris for competition. It was immediately successful and went into production. As the cars were built in the Morris garage, they were named MG, for Morris Garage. William Morris began acquiring other British car companies (Riley, Woolsley, etc.), forming the Nuffield Corporation.

Shortly after the end of WW II, a few MG TCs were imported into the United States by J. S. Inskip in New York and by Kjell Qvale (British Motor Car Distributors) and International Motors on the West Coast.

In 1956, the Hambro Trading Company was formed to purchase cars from Nuffield for shipment and distribution to the United States. Gough Industries, distributors of Philco radios, televisions and refrigerators, handled distribution in California. They were pretty hang-loose, appointing used car dealers (with no service facilities) as MG dealers. Later, Gough allowed Qvale to take over distribution in Northern California.

In 1952, Nuffield and Austin merged, forming the British Motor Corporation, headed by Leonard Lord. In 1966, Jaguar merged with BMC, which was renamed British Motor Holdings. Leyland, an old British company dating back to 1895, became the largest British manufacturer of cars and commercial vehicles, eventually acquiring, among others, MG, Austin, Austin Healey, Jaguar and Rover. In 1968, the British Leyland Motor Corp. (BLMC) was formed. In 1978, MG became part newly-formed Jaguar-Rover-Triumph (JRT). Amid worldwide protests by MG dealers and enthusiasts, on 24 October, 1980, the MG factory closed its doors on fifty years of history.

4   The Davis Car

H ave you ever heard of the Davis Car?
In 1948, Gary Davis designed a three-wheel car, to be constructed in a rented 57,000 square-foot building in Van Nuys, California. He sold over 300 franchises for more than 1.2 million dollars, and proceeded to build his innovative three-wheel car.

Davis ultimately completed 17 cars, of which 12 exist today, before being indicted for fraud. He served two years in the hoosegow. (Actually, it was a very good car for the period and it was a shame the project failed – sound a bit like the Tucker?)

The Davis facility included a test track, a short road course with a few turns. As a publicity stunt, Davis put on, and publicized, a weeklong economy run, the idea being that one or two Davis cars would compete against any other entrants. The only response came from International Motors. Roger Barlow sent two cars to compete: a 1948 MG TC and a 1948 Renault 4cv. As I was currently unemployed, I was happy to accept Roger's offer of fifty bucks to drive for the week.

It was an enjoyable seven days. I brought a sleeping bag and camped on the factory floor most nights. Mobil sent a tanker truck for the week. Probably due to a lack of publicity, not too many people came to watch, so we ran the cars around during the day and early evening, but never for 24 hours at a time, as originally planned.

There were several other drivers during the week, including Jack Early, Bernard Cahier and Phil Hill.

In conjunction with the Economy Run, two Sundays were devoted to time trials, with a wide assortment of sports cars competing for a fast time around the track.

When we got good and bored, we played games with the cars (not very fast, only about fifteen miles an hour).

Daredevil Moss at (slow) speed.

Gary signed this picture for me. Here the two of us are chatting.

5   A Car Club is Born

One reason I wanted an MG was that I'd been reading about trials and rallies being held in England, and I thought such events would be lots of fun. I quickly discovered that no such activities were taking place on the West Coast, so I organized the first rally held in Southern California. I had recently met several car enthusiasts and they were happy to participate. This event took place on January 16th, 1949, and went from Los Angeles to Santa Barbara. It was a time/speed/distance event, with five "legs" and five check points. A time/speed/distance (TSD) rally requires the driver and navigator to negotiate each leg at a given average speed, being docked for being early or late at a checkpoint.

The cars entered included: thirteen MG TCs, a British Talbot, an Ulster Aston Martin, a Mark IV Jaguar, a Riley, a Bristol, and two American cars. Among the participants were Keenan Wynn, Larry Parks, in his TC, and Tom Bamford, all of whom were experts at similar events on their motorcycles. The surprise winners were Ed & Lotus Jacobs, in their MG TC. They knew from nothing about a rally – they just drove, stopped for candy bars, and had the best score!

Following this event, I called a meeting at my house and a club was formed. On the advice of an attorney/member, we named it the Foreign Car Group, as he felt being a non-club could absolve us of any liability in case of an accident.

To celebrate Memorial Day, several club members in seven TCs journeyed from Los Angeles to Ensenada, Mexico, for the three-day weekend. When we arrived in Ensenada, one couple announced they going to be married and I was to be the best man. I accompanied the groom-to-

be to the city hall, where a few pesos excused him from having a blood test. While I was waiting, I entered my name in the big *Book of Mexican Births*. Does this make me an illegal alien?

It was quite a weekend, with one TC being impounded, due to the one and only motor cop running over a wastebasket he assumed the driver had thrown at him. Truth was, I had dropped the wastebasket out of a second-story hotel room window in order to attract the driver's attention! Fortunately, we had become friends with the mayor and, after rousing His Honor from his bed, he ordered the release of the MG.

Another TC adventure was in September of 1949, when Joan Fetterman and I eloped to Las Vegas in the TC. We were joined by five other TCs and, with our friends, had a most enjoyable honeymoon! The night that we were married, we attended one of Liberace's performances and he dedicated a song to the newlyweds – us.

Not long after Joan and I married, a significant tragedy occurred. Against my protestations, the Foreign Car Group arranged a day of time trials at Muroc Dry Lake. These were high-speed, one car at a time races against the clock, over a one-mile course on the salt bed, marked by very few rubber cones. Early in the day, Jim Pray rolled his TC and, although not badly injured, was taken to the hospital.

A short time later, the event organizer, recently married Jack Fancher, rolled his TC in a high-speed turn and was thrown out, landing on his head. He died on the way to the hospital. Jack and his wife Joan were our very good friends and I was a pallbearer at his rainy funeral, conducted by the same minister who had married him not long before.

The Foreign Car Group survived for several more years, putting on rallies and funkhanas.

What is a funkhana? A funkhana consists of various driving skill events, always at slow speeds. A blindfold-driving test is a popular event. In this event, the driver is blindfolded and the passenger directs him (or her) through a course marked by rubber cones – driving partly forward and partly in reverse. This is always good for a few laughs, with the passenger, usually the wife, either *pointing* to the desired direction, or saying, "No, the *OTHER* way!" (See photos on the next page).

An offshoot of the Foreign Car Group was the Long Beach MG Club. Dottie and Dan Dickinson grew tired of driving the thirty-five miles from Long Beach to attend the meetings of the FCG in Los Angeles, so they called a meeting at the home of John de Friest and a new club was formed – the Long Beach MG Club. This is still a very active club, but with very few member's MGs.

A few years ago I drove my MG TC from Sedona to Long Beach for the fiftieth anniversary of the LBMG Club. I had practically the only MG there, certainly the only TC. Progress?

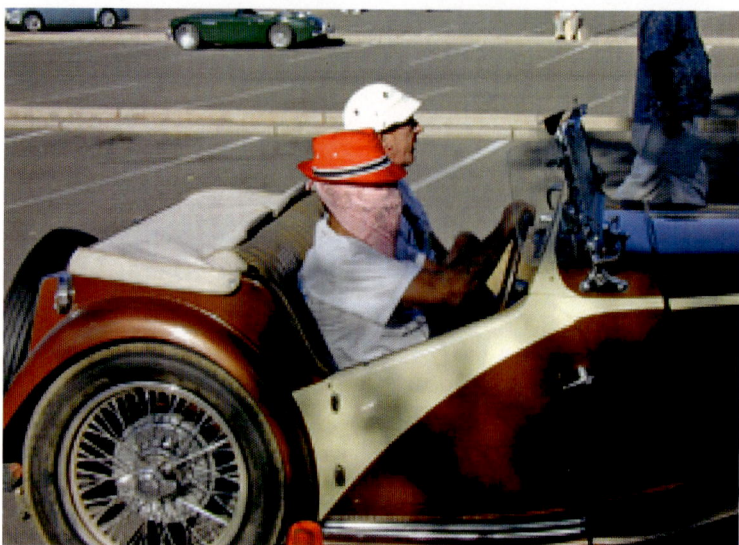

Blindfold driving in a funkhana.

🌀 6   The Birth of Moss Motors

hortly after the Foreign Car Group was organized, I became aware that many MG owners were dissatisfied with the service, or lack thereof, available in the L.A. area. Since I was currently unemployed, and had done considerable exploratory surgery on my TC, I decided to open my own shop. Early in 1949, I rented space at Jack Gilchrist's new garage at 3200 West Olympic Boulevard, where I opened my first shop, specializing in MG repair and general wheel alignment.

I worked strictly by myself and soon had built up a clientele base of mostly MG TC customers, along with a few owners of other British cars. I enjoyed having my own business. Occasionally, in mid-afternoon, I would close the doors and a few of us would take off for a tour in the surrounding mountains or along the ocean.

Beginning with a few tools, a hydraulic floor jack and a welding outfit, I soon purchased a set of wheel alignment instruments from Bagge & Son. With no inventory, every time I did a job and needed parts, I would duplicate the order and stock the balance. Every penny of profit was invested in tools, equipment and inventory.

Early on, I did no advertising, had no sign on the building, or a name for the business. My customer base was built both by word of mouth and by parking my MG and customer cars in sight of busy Olympic Boulevard.

There were several used car lots in the vicinity selling new MG TCs, but with no service facilities. I made arrangements to pick up their new TCs and do the set-up and initial servicing. After these cars were sold, many of the new owners became regular customers.

I was happy operating this small shop and was able to support my wife and myself, although Joan did supplement our income by working as a nurse.

In 1952, I was offered the opportunity, through a family member, to close the shop, move to the Midwest and attend the General Motors Training School. Upon "graduation," I would have assumed the position of service manager for a large Oldsmobile agency in Iowa. Considering the fact that I had no college degree, this was probably the best situation I could have hoped to achieve in the automotive trade.

Joan and I considered this offer from all angles – leaving California for the hot and humid Midwestern summers, and the bitter, cold, snowy winters, and decided to remain where we were. I have never regretted that decision.

*   *   *   *

COMPLETE MG SERVICE

* Factory Parts
* Accessories
* Lubrication
* Tune-up
* Complete Overhaul
* Wheel Alignment

E. ALAN MOSS
3200 W. Olympic Blvd.
(2 Blks. East of Western)
Los Angeles 6, Calif.
REpublic 3-1775
(*All Work Guaranteed*)

My first ad. September, 1949, Motor Trend.

7 M.M.L. & B.R.S.

After establishing my first shop, I only worked half a day on Saturday, closed up shop, and went to lunch with fellow car nuts who dropped by to chat, look at the cars, and perhaps have a tune-up or a bit of work done.

Sometimes there might be eight or ten of us, sometimes three or four. These were not necessarily customers, just friends and hangers-on. The Taylor brothers, Roy and Dudley, regularly drove one or both of their TCs all the way from Riverside to join us for lunch.

One of the regulars was Ben Sears, a TD owner and a commercial artist by trade. There was no membership, but Ben created the name, "Moss Motors Luncheon and Bench Racing Society," and designed an appropriate badge. We made twenty-five of these badges and sold them to the "non-members" for a buck each. We proudly displayed them on the front of our MGs, or in Dr. John Benton's case, his Morgan.

For the uninitiated, the term "bench racing" refers to what all drivers and would-be drivers do off the track: "I woulda won that race if only. . ."

The badge is very clever and has remained exclusive to the original non-members. A few years ago an attempt was made to reproduce and sell them to the public. Help from an attorney aided me in putting a stop to this. I personally cannot see why anyone would buy and display any badge from a club or group to which they never belonged.

The Badge

8   Allard Days

At the beginning of 1950, I had an opportunity to get into the automobile sales business and decided to import a line of British cars. The only marque which was not presently being imported on the West Coast, was Allard. This appeared to be a viable prospect – a well-respected (in England) line of high-powered sports cars, using Ford V-8 engines and driveline components. I established a relationship with Sydney Allard, whereby I would be the exclusive West Coast Allard importer and distributor for the entire line of cars. Previously, Roy Richter, the owner of Bell Auto Parts, had expressed interest in importing only the J-2 Competition model, so we shared distribution of this model.

I made arrangements with the Ford Motor Company to purchase small quantities of new Ford and Mercury V8 engines, and bought complete, crated engines for about $150 each.

I promptly placed an order for a K-model Allard, a very attractive two-seater roadster fitted with the English version of the American 85-horsepower, flathead-Ford engine. While the car was "on the water," I had my friend Vic Edelbrock build a modified Mercury engine. The car arrived in Los Angeles in time for me to install this engine and prepare the car for the first Southern California road race, held in Palm Springs on April 15-16, 1950.

My friend, and soon-to-be sales manager, Tom Frisbey was entered to drive the car. Race weekend proved to be unbearably hot and the flathead Mercury engine boiled constantly. Even though we had the fastest car, and led the main event for a while, we were forced to slow with a blown head gasket. Sterling Edwards in his V8-60-powered Edwards Special won the race.

21

Notice steam from the right exhaust pipe due to a blown head gasket.
(Palm Springs. April, 1950)   Photo-Morgan Sinclair

A few months later, I placed an order for a bright red J-2 Competition model Allard, set up for the recently-released Kettering-Cadillac OHV (overhead valve) engine. I modified this new engine with solid lifters, an Edmonds dual carb manifold, Mallory ignition, and exhaust headers, raising the horsepower from 160 to over 180.

The car arrived from England in time for me to install this engine and do a bit of road testing, naturally on Mulholland Drive. I drove the car to Carmel for the first running of the Pebble Beach Road Races in November, 1950. I had nominated Englishman Michael Graham to be the driver and had assembled a competent, well-trained timing and scoring team – or so I thought.

A few minor problems developed during practice, but I had these sorted out in time for the preliminary race, the Monterey Cup, which Michael won handily. This gave us a front row position for the start of the main event, the Pebble Beach Cup. Just before the flag fell to start the race

I noticed water coming out of the radiator overflow pipe. As this engine always ran quite cool, I was quite concerned, but could do nothing until Graham pulled into our pit at the end of the first lap. Whipping open the hood, I immediately noticed that the narrow fan belt had come off. While I was attempting to reinstall the belt, Big Jack McAfee took over and installed the belt *with his bare hands*! After replenishing the radiator water, we sent Michael back to join the fray. Try as he might, even though he passed most of the field, he could finish no higher than third position – not too bad for our second racing effort. The poor little Ford clutch just wasn't up to the Caddy's torque. It was slipping so badly that, after the race, I was unable to drive the car up the main street of Carmel, let alone back to Los Angeles. Luckily, I had brought a trailer along.

For you unfortunate readers who never had the privilege of attending any of the seven Pebble Beach road races (1950-56) – please believe me when I tell you that there has never been anything like these since, at least not on the West Coast. The sight and sound of the cars, especially those with large-displacement engines, ripping through the tree-lined turns and narrow straights was indescribable. The first time the pack came screaming by the pits, with our Allard way out in front, my well-trained scoring team just sat there wide-eyed and open-mouthed. So much for our timing and scoring!

*   *   *   *

I finally made the comic pages! The following ad for Royal Triton motor oil appeared in the *Los Angeles Times* Sunday funnies on April 22nd, 1951. It says, in part, "E. Alan Moss, Western Distributor for Allard, says, 'I recommend Royal Triton motor oil for the Allard because

it gives extra protection to precision-built engines.'"
Hogwash! I wouldn't use the stuff and gave the two free
cases to my mother-in-law to use in her Chevrolet!

(In all fairness, this purple-color, detergent, oil was OK,
but *only* when used in a completely clean engine; it did not
mix well with other oils)

This ad appeared in the Los Angeles Times, April 22, 1951.

A few very dated publicity shots
of my first K-type Allard.
My, don't I look young? I was!

During the winter months, I made some modifications to the Allard and decided to enter it in a February 27th, 1951, California Sports Car Club event at the Carrell Speedway half-mile dirt track, with myself as driver. Rain fell heavily all night prior to race day and the track was a sea of mud when we arrived. The rain let up, so we spent several hours wheel-packing the track. The program started with a Trophy Dash (three laps for the three fastest qualifiers). I had the second-fastest qualifying time and started in the middle, between Phil Hill in his 2.9 Alfa and Bud Satcher in his ex-Indy two-man car. The starter waved the green flag, and guess who forgot to put his Allard in gear? If I had raised my hand, we would have had a restart. But, there are no "ifs" in motor racing!

Now, we come to the main event. As this was an inverted start (fastest cars in the rear), I started at the very back of the pack, and the slowest car, Henry Manney in his red Crosley Hotshot, started in front. When the flag fell, starting in 2nd gear, I shot past the whole field like a scalded cat and was in first position coming out of the second turn. I led for one lap, and at the start of the second lap, I glanced back and saw a red car approaching and thought *if that's Henry's Hotshot, I am not going fast enough.* I floored the accelerator, and the car slid down into the muddy infield. As it turned out, the red car was Bud Satcher's ex-Indy car, and he was attempting to pass my sliding Allard. We touched, the Allard bit into the mud, and began cartwheeling down the backstretch. After 2-1/2 very high flips, the car landed upside down, with me pinned underneath. I was knocked unconscious, probably on the first flip, and hung from the seat belt each time the car was high in the air. Fortunately, there was no fire and, considering that the car had no roll bar, I was one lucky pup.

Most of my serious injuries were from straining against the seat belt. Fortunately, my car never landed on me. I was wearing Keenan Wynn's metal, motorcycle crash-helmet; we later learned that a metal helmet could be very dangerous. My head hit the track surface hard enough to imbed dirt into the helmet, but not dent it (or my skull).

This was one spectacular racing accident and was captured on film and shown that evening on the L.A. news broadcasts. This accident, and much of the day's racing, is shown on my DVD set, *Films of the Fabulous Fifties*.

During my week in the hospital, I had many visitors, including friends from the California Sports Car Club. Henry Manney stopped by and told me, "I passed beneath a flying racecar, looked up and said to myself, 'Hmmm, deDion rear end – must be Moss.'" (A feature of the Allard was the unique deDion rear suspension system.)

Following this harrowing experience, I came to the conclusion that racing was against my religion; I am an Orthodox Coward!

*   *   *   *

On the following page are a few very poor pictures of the wreck. The poor quality is due to the fact that they are taken from a fifty-eight year-old copy of a copy of a 16mm film.

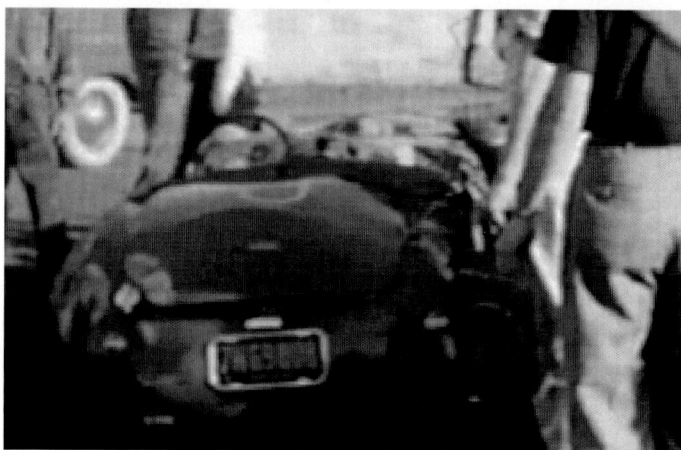

Prior to the race, I installed a screen at the front to protect the paint.
That was the only part of the car that remained undamaged!

⑨ Dealership Woos

When I became the Allard distributor in 1950, I rented more shop space and a showroom from my landlord, Jack Gilchrist. Soon it became necessary to take on another line of cars to fill up the space. I therefore became the first Rootes dealer in Los Angeles. Rootes Motors was sort of the General Motors of Great Britain, producing Sunbeam-Talbot, Hillman Minx, Commer, Singer and Humber, as well as other makes. This came at the time of the Korean War energy crunch, and all of a sudden "small" cars, such as Hillman Minx and Austin, were in demand. I quickly was forced into learning (don't forget, I was just a kid of twenty-four) the dark and filthy side of the Automobile Game.

We had a batch of orders, with deposits, for Hillmans, but were unable to get any cars out of Rootes Motors. We began having our customers request refunds and, after a bit of sleuthing, I found that Peter Satori, the Beverly Hills Rootes distributor, had set up one of his employees with a dealer license and this man was delivering Hillmans out of a storage garage located a few miles from my establishment and definitely in my defined territory. The head of the Rootes West Coast operation would send a prospective customer to the above-mentioned garage, where a new Hillman could be purchased and delivered immediately. Of course, Mr. Head Man pocketed most of the difference between the cost and selling price.

On at least one occasion, Mr. Head Man sent a prospective customer to my agency with the understanding that I would reimburse him (Mr. H.M.), in cash of course, one-half of my profit. When I went to complain to Rootes

headquarters, I was dismayed to discover that my Rootes contract had been stolen from a locked cabinet. Such are the joys of trying to run a legitimate business.

About this time, Mr. Head Man (whose initials, incidentally, were H. H.), along with a partner, opened a Rootes agency in Westchester, near Los Angeles International Airport. This was just like any other automobile agency, with one big exception – all cars were sold at 100% profit. Seems that Mr. Head Man was "uninventorying" them from Rootes stock. When the ax fell, he hopped a plane for South America, while his partner went to prison. I began wondering if it was even possible to make an honest living selling cars!

After this episode, and my Allard accident, I came very close to bankruptcy. Upon partially recovering from my accident, I rented a small space behind an Associated Gasoline station at 4675 West Pico Boulevard, and was slowly able to get back on my feet repairing cars.

One happier day, while lying in my hospital bed at home, I received *two* phone calls from people wanting to order Allards, both black K-2s, to be fitted with Cadillac engines. By the time the cars arrived in Los Angeles, I was well enough to install the engines. As I had to deliver the cars, one to Albuquerque and the other to Houston, I prevailed upon my good friend Dan Dickinson to drive one car as far as Albuquerque and fly home. I continued alone to Houston. The cars ran faultlessly and created quite a stir along the way.

Dan and I ready to leave for Albuquerque and Houston. Notice the water bag. That's my J2 in the shop.

When we stopped and raised the hoods to check the oil, people gathered around and saw *Cadillac* emblazoned on the valve covers. They always asked what kind of cars they were. We told them they were new, secret, experimental model Cadillacs and not to tell anyone they saw them. We would exit with lots of wheel spin, and, once out of sight, settle down to a reasonable cruising speed. After all, neither car was yet paid for!

Upon my return from Texas, I set about rebuilding my wrecked Cad-Allard. I ordered a new tail section from England and had top race car builder, Emil Diedt, repair the rest of the damage. As there was no frame damage, the car came out like new when it was finished. It was sold to Bill Carmen, who raced it in several California races.

During the brief course of my venture into the auto sales world, I sold perhaps a dozen Allards. While I thought the J-2 was a great, well-priced, all-around sports car, the rest of the line stunk as far as I was concerned. Their big claim to fame was the fitting of various large American engines (Ford, Mercury, Cadillac, Oldsmobile, Chrysler, etc.). The night I sold my last Allard, I went out and purchased a Jaguar XK-120 roadster. What does that tell you!

*   *   *   *

After two years of suffering in the aforementioned tiny shop, with only a metal grate to keep out the wind and rain, I managed to locate and purchase a suitable vacant lot at 5776 Venice Boulevard, near Culver City. A contractor friend, Howard Friedman, then constructed a neat concrete block building for me.

10 A New Moss Motors Home

At last, I had a large, comfortable, new shop of my very own.

I had a succession of apprentice mechanics and during construction of the new shop; a young fellow just out of high school came to work for me. His name was Michael Goodman. Mike stayed with me through thick and thin and eventually ended up with the shop and repair business on Venice Boulevard when I moved to Santa Barbara in 1963. Mike and I remain good friends to this day.

Shortly after moving into my new shop, Ken Miles, the service manager for Gough Industries (the Southern California MG distributor), appointed me an MG Service Dealer. This meant that I enjoyed all of the privileges of a regular dealer (a discount on parts, all service bulletins, doing warranty work, etc.), other than selling new cars.

Soon after becoming an MG service dealer, Charles Hornburg (the Jaguar distributor), appointed my shop as the first, factory-authorized, Jaguar service dealership in Los Angeles, with the same privileges offered by MG. After complying with Hornburg's demands that I purchase a fairly large stock of Jaguar parts, it wasn't long before he canceled my service dealership, leaving me to wonder if he just wanted to make a large parts sale! However, my shop continued servicing Jaguar cars, and I was still able to purchase parts at a small discount.

While we worked on many makes of imported cars, we specialized in MG, Jaguar and Austin Healey. It was also my pleasure to service, and do major work on, several late 1930s classic Rolls-Bentley cars.

The last of the T-Series MGs were built in 1955, at which time the MGA series was introduced. Shortly thereafter, the MG factory discontinued manufacturing

and supplying parts for the T-Series MGs – cars which had been in production since before the war.

I maintained a comprehensive stock of MG parts and, thanks to a referral in *Road & Track*, I began receiving inquiries from all over the world about parts availability. People began asking about a catalog. Did I have one? Why not produce one? When will one be available?

So, being an amateur photographer, with good equipment and a permanent darkroom, I began work on a catalog. I spread a white sheet on the floor, placed an assortment of parts on the sheet, stood on a ladder and photographed the parts. After printing the photographs, I typed all the descriptions and prices on a $35 typewriter. The finished product was a neat, 28-page, illustrated, T-Series parts catalog that we mailed all over the world. I followed this up with a similar catalog for the MGA.

As I was devoting most of my time to the burgeoning parts business, I took Mike Goodman in as a partner in the shop. By this time he was a very competent mechanic, having attended the MG and Jaguar service schools and possessing a natural talent for this work.

Mike and I had many laughs during those times. We worked hard, but managed to find time for occasional fun and games. Venice Boulevard is a busy thoroughfare and people often wanted to use the shop telephone when they had a breakdown or ran out of gas nearby. I finally had a pay phone installed inside the shop, with a "telephone" sign outside. Hanging next to the phone was a binder containing two phone books. However, the white pages were from Mexico City and the classified pages from Greater Brooklyn. We got our kicks by watching some poor soul trying to call the local Auto Club for help! On top of that, all our phones, including the pay phone, had plain white dials, with no numbers or letters.

During construction of the new building, I silver-soldered a small assortment of coins to large nails and had them placed in the wet concrete floor, in front of the showcase. Customers paying their bills would try in vain to pick up the coins.

The intersection adjacent to the shop always contained a couple of inches of water during a rainstorm. We considered obtaining a bunch of sawhorses and cutting them down a few inches progressively and placing them through the intersection during a heavy rain. Who would dare drive into an area with only two inches of sawhorse showing! We never got around to doing this, but had many laughs thinking and talking about it.

One of the duties of a new apprentice was to lower the overhead garage doors each day at closing time. Every few days, we would shorten the pull ropes an inch. Pretty soon the poor guy was looking for something to stand on to reach the ropes. It took awhile for him to figure out what was happening.

I had many fortunate opportunities to purchase from numerous dealers both large and small stocks of what had become obsolete MG parts. One purchase was a huge load directly from BMC, consisting of unopened crates of new parts that had come over with the original MG shipments – parts that were currently listed by them as NLS (No Longer Supplied).

I also purchased stocks from International Motors, Bering Monroe Motors, Pete Rabuzzi Motors, S. H. Arnolt in Chicago, Cavalier Motors, British Leyland, and even a large supply from Innocenti Motors in Italy.

I was dismayed one day to see on the dock at the MG importers (BMC in Compton), a stack of new TD front

fenders I was told were being scrapped. They refused to sell them to me at any price, explaining, "We want to get all those old cars (MGs, etc.) off the road and sell the owners new MG 1100s." My response was that the owners of MGs would keep them going no matter what. and the last thing they will buy is an MG 1100!

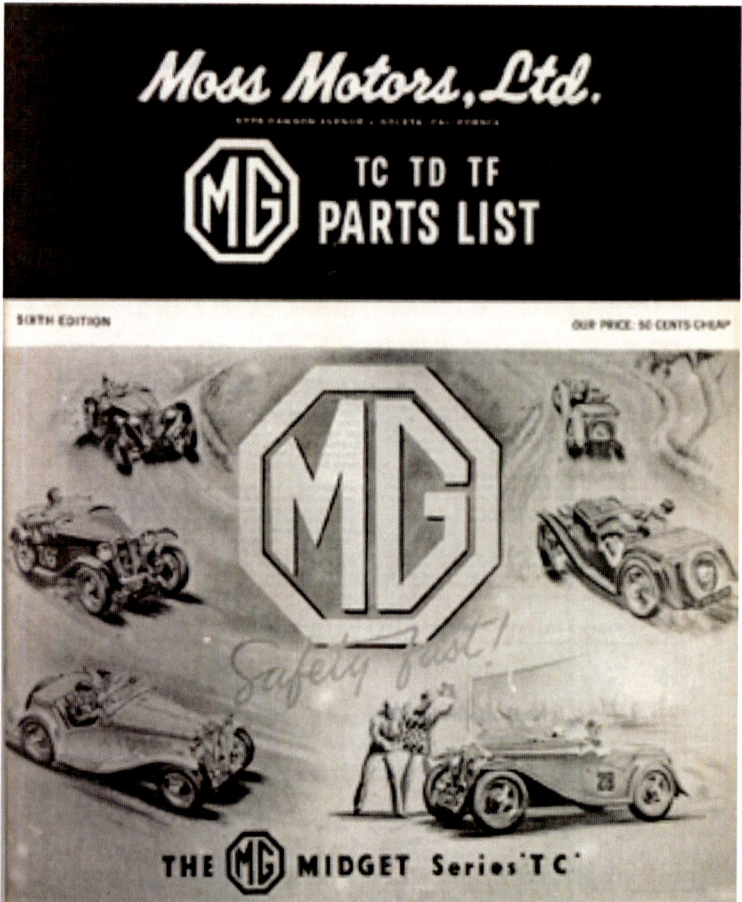

The cover of my first MG T-Series catalog.

11 Moss Motors Moves Again

In the early 1960s, Joan and I decided Los Angeles was becoming a less than desirable place to raise our children and decided to relocate. I purchased a vacant lot on a side street in Goleta, a pleasant suburb of Santa Barbara. Mike Goodman and his wife, Sharon, did not wish to leave Los Angeles, so we dissolved the partnership and I began construction of a new home for Moss Motors.

Since there was an MG agency located in Santa Barbara (Claude Phipps Motors), I met with John Beazley and Ken Miles, manager and service manager respectively, of what was then called British Motors Corporation (BMC), importers of MG, Austin Healey, etc. I obtained their permission to continue selling parts by mail after we moved, providing I did not solicit any local sales.

Joan and I put our Los Angeles house on the market and, fortunately, it sold the first day it was offered. Then began the Big Move. We rented a nice house in Santa Barbara, and packed all the tools, parts and household belongings for the movers to transport to Santa Barbara. The next thing we knew we were in Santa Barbara: kids, dog, cats and all, ready to start a new life and a new business.

I was just getting started in the mail order parts business on a full-time basis. In order to supplement our income, I took on a jobbership with Lucas, Beck-Arnley and BAP (British Auto Parts), distributing complete lines of parts for all imported cars to shops and dealerships in the Tri-Counties area (Santa Barbara, Ventura and San Luis Obispo counties).

In March of 1963, the family and I moved into the rented house, and Moss Motors occupied the nearly completed store. The first few days were hectic, what with unpacking parts and filling orders, without electricity. But we got settled and were quite happy in our surroundings.

37

Note my London Taxi — a Beardmore.

The business did well. We had a delivery truck, a full time outside salesman, and ultimately, three satellite stores – one in Goleta, one in downtown Santa Barbara and one a hundred miles north in San Luis Obispo.

Not long after the new store was opened, I invited Claude Phipps, owner of the Santa Barbara MG agency, for a tour. While we chatted in my office, I carefully explained our purpose was to keep supplying parts for old British cars, primarily on a mail order basis, and would not interfere with his business.

We ended on what I thought was a friendly note. Phipps then drove directly to Compton and tried to get my franchise cancelled. By this time, Kjell Qvale (British Motor Car Distributors) had taken over the importation and distribution of BMC cars. I made an appointment with Kjell, flew to San Francisco, and had a serious meeting with Kjell and his general manager, Andy Regalia, during which I pled my case, explaining that we were filling a gap which no one else was willing to do, by continuing to stock,

manufacture and supply parts for obsolete BMC cars. I assured these gentlemen that we did not, and would not, sell any parts for current BMC cars locally, and would not do anything to detract from Claude Phipps' parts sales.

Kjell and Andy listened to my explanation and very graciously agreed to allow me to continue. I felt they were very fair. Kjell was, and is to this day, a true car enthusiast and a good friend, who has never forgotten it was an MG TC that got him started in business many, many years ago.

On at least two occasions, with no prior notification, I was paid an early morning visit by a fellow from BMC/Compton, who spent most of the day going through stacks of our sales invoices, trying to catch us selling any forbidden BMC parts locally. Needless to say, he found none.

Ultimately, the whole thing backfired on Phipps. The local repair shops, while aware that we had a huge stock of parts, were forced to go downtown to Phipps's establishment, only to be told that he didn't have the parts in question and was unable to obtain them.

In 1968, I began making trips to England and succeeded in establishing relationships with some large companies, such as Lockheed (brake parts), Borg & Beck (clutches), Payen (gaskets), Morris Garages, Armstrong Shock Absorbers, etc. and was able to purchase parts directly. I also contracted with several companies to have obsolete parts manufactured. It did not take long for me to discover the typical British lack of incentive:

"How is business?"

"Terrible."

"Where are the orders I placed with you a year ago?"

"Well, we've been on holiday, you know."

I thoroughly enjoyed making trips to England, usually one or two each year. I made quite a few good friends and was invited into many homes. Contrary to most American visitors, I enjoyed the English food and strong coffee. The countryside is beautiful and green and the people, very friendly. I had the opportunity of attending several motor races and visiting many car and motorcycle museums. I also made a few trips into Scotland.

In addition, I traveled to South Africa, where laws prevented the import of foreign cars. Cars had to be made locally, using a very high content of locally manufactured parts. As British Leyland S. A. had discontinued manufacturing MGs, Healeys, and older model Jaguars, I was invited to purchase their stock of parts for these obsolete models.

I flew from London to Nairobi, Kenya, and spent two days there, renting a small Datsun to drive to the Amboseli Game Preserve. This is a long trip and I drove way too fast on the rough, washboard, unpaved, roads and nearly destroyed the car. Fortunately, my camera had a long lens and I was able to get some nice wild animal photos.

I flew from Nairobi to Cape Town, and was treated royally by British Leyland's top brass, who invited me to the introduction of their new Rover model. At this gala reception, I met some interesting car enthusiasts. I truly fell in love with the area and was sad when it came time to leave. I'd love to go back to South Africa someday.

Meanwhile, back in California, Moss Motors was having trouble getting many needed parts, so I decided to build a machine shop on the property.

Things went on swimmingly at Moss Motors, until I discovered that our satellite stores, despite having a good crew and enjoying ample sales, were costing my company thousands of dollars each month, which my highly paid Beverly Hills accountants did not pick up. After trying unsuccessfully to restore this part of our operation to good

health, I sold that part of the business to BAP-GEON.

Moss Motors basic business of manufacturing and supplying parts for MG, Jaguar, Healey and Triumph was healthy and growing. However, we were completely out of space, even though we had expanded the building two times. In desperation, I purchased three acres of vacant land on Hollister Avenue, the main street in Goleta, and built a new, two-story building. About that time, an opportunity presented itself to sell the entire operation to Howard Goldman. I had several reasons for deciding to sell. With nearly sixty employees, running the business was no longer enjoyable, and my first wife, Joan, who was half-owner of the corporation, and vital to the operation, (being in charge of accounting and office procedures), wanted to retire. If she had done so, I would have had to take charge of all her duties, in addition to my own.

So, in 1977, at the ripe old age of fifty, I sold out and retired. I had a nice home in Hope Ranch (Santa Barbara), with a big garage and a stable. I began restoring cars as a hobby. Over the next few years, I restored several MGs, a LeMans Healey-100, a Jaguar XK-140 MC roadster, Old Number Eleven, and an MGB roadster.

Anyway, after taking control of Moss Motors, Goldman began to expand the company, establishing branches in the East and in England, as well as expanding from old British cars to supplying parts and accessories for a broad range of domestic and imported cars. Compared to when I owned the company, Moss Motors has become *HUGE*!

*   *   *   *

Along with many trials and tribulations through the years, I do have some humorous memories from my Moss Motors days, a few of which follow.

Moss Motors received periodic price updates from the various manufacturers. Shortly after we received a new price book from BMC, a customer phoned and asked if I had a certain MG part in stock. When I replied in the affirmative, he asked the price. I looked in the new price book and quoted him the price, which was $49.85. He told me that his local dealer only wanted $42.55 (the old price). When I asked why he didn't buy the part there, he told me that they were out of the item. "Gee," I said, "When we are out of that part, we only charge $25.00."

One day a customer called, complaining that we sent the wrong part, which did not match the picture in our catalog. I patiently explained that if he were to take his car out of the garage and back it in, the part would fit perfectly!

Another time, one of my parts men inadvertently sent an extra part in a shipment. I wrote the customer and suggested he either return the part at our expense or pay for it at a discount. His father wrote back, saying they were going to keep the part. I wrote to him saying, "If you are trying to teach your son to be a crook, you are doing a good job. Keep the part." The next time the kid sent a check to order more parts, I cashed the check and thanked him for paying for the extra part he had previously received.

*   *   *   *

As my granddad used to say, "Why are there more horses asses than there are horses?"

12 The Fabulous Fifties

Those of us who were fortunate to "be there" and to be involved in the early days of sports car road racing in California in the 1950s, whether as drivers, officials or spectators, will always remember that era as The Fabulous Fifties: a time when the cars ran on skinny tires, the drivers wore T-shirts and many race cars were driven to (and hopefully from) the events. The courses consisted of whatever could be found: streets, airports, abandoned military posts – whatever. By and large, we were a close-knit and friendly group. It didn't matter whether you could barely afford the entry fee or were very wealthy, as some were.

*   *   *   *

Following recovery from my racing accident, I did no more serious competition driving, but remained active in the sport in various official capacities. I began my career in officialdom as pit steward, and later took over technical inspection, finally becoming chief race judge. In addition, I served on the contest board for several years. I also enjoyed preparing a few cars for competition and crewing for various drivers.

My activities as pit steward involved assigning pits for each race, and, during race weekend, "policing" the pit area to keep out any unauthorized persons.

When there was an opening for someone to head up technical inspection, I accepted that job. This involved organizing a team of competent mechanics to examine all cars prior to each race. We had to make sure the cars met the various requirements: operating lights, horn, emergency brake, spare wheel, proper engine size, etc. All production cars had to be absolutely stock, except for the removal of bumpers, windscreens and hubcaps.

In order to avoid the delays and congestion caused by Saturday morning tech inspection at the track, I devised a plan whereby we would hold tech inspections two evenings during the week prior to a race. Owners of shops and agencies were happy to help. I had a team of tech inspectors; all the shop or agency had to provide was space, floor jacks and, usually, coffee and donuts. This proved to be a satisfactory arrangement; Saturday inspections were reserved for out of town entrants, and to recheck defects that were found earlier.

Most of the problems (and cheating) occurred in the production classes. My first contact with Ken Miles was at a Torrey Pines race, where he showed up with a "stock" MG TD, owned by the importer. Ken had removed all of the interior upholstery. An argument ensued. Ken claimed it didn't make any difference but I said, "If not, then why was it removed?" I won. Ken replaced the interior, and we remained friends.

On two occasions, I had the unmitigated gall to raise a hood on the starting line, only to discover that a previously-rejected item had been reinstalled. One driver was so mad, he actually tried to run over me with his car.

In December 1952, a cold, practice day at Torrey Pines, up came Johnny von Neumann, twenty-five dollars in hand, to file a formal protest against Ernie McAfee's SIATA race car.

Ernie had purchased the rights to the Barker engine and was producing them in small quantities. The Barker, a copy of the Offenhauser engine, was designed for use in midget auto racing cars and, as such, had a displacement of 96.9 cubic inches, which put it 88 cc over the 1500 cc class limit.

Johnny proceeded to tell me that his "shpies kept vatch on Ernie's shop and the SIATA vus not moofed from

under itz tarp sinze der last raze, vere it vuz undoubtedly oversize." I told Johnny I didn't want to know any of this and sealed the engine to make it tamperproof, thus allowing Ernie to race the car all weekend.

A few days after the race, John's representative, the local press and yours truly converged on Ernie's shop. I came armed with a beaker and the brainstorm of measuring the capacity of the engine by pouring a measured amount of oil through a spark plug hole, thereby calculating the total displacement of the engine. This was a nice idea in theory, however it failed, due to the liquid seeping past the piston rings.

The next step was for Ernie to remove the entire cylinder block (like an Offenhauser engine, the head and block are one casting). Ernie was quite cheerful, and it wasn't long before the engine was stripped bare. I was then able to accurately measure and determine the displacement.

As I expected, the displacement was absolutely correct.

After all of the hangers-on and the press left, Ernie told me the whole story.

Yes, the engine *had been* oversize and he knew Johnny's "shpies" had kept a close vigil, but not close enough! Early one morning, about 3 A.M., they pulled the car inside the shop and quickly replaced the entire engine with an identical engine, but with a new, "destroked" crankshaft, which brought the engine within specifications.

Ernie had the last laugh on Johnny!

* * * *

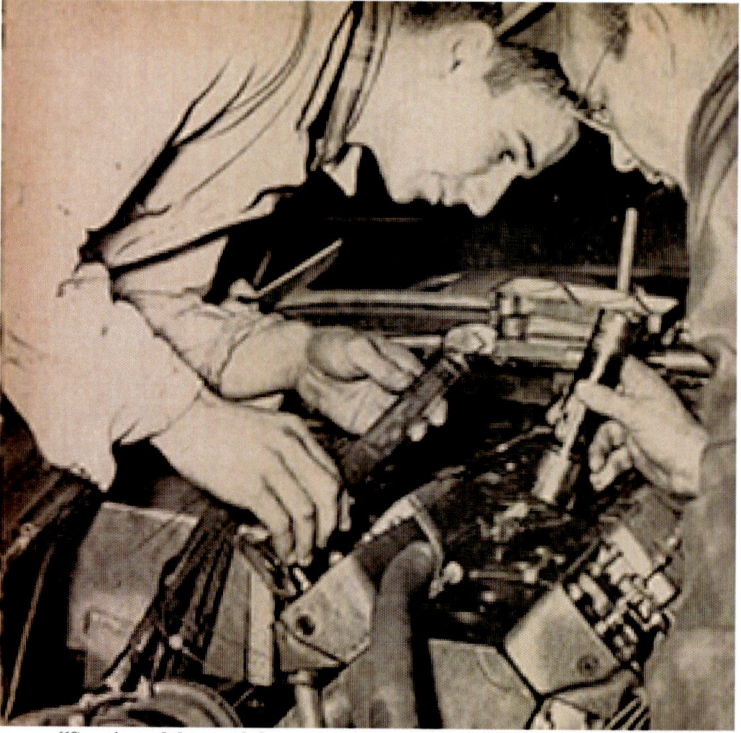

"Scrutineer Moss and Owner McAfee try measuring the engine using oil."

After a stint as chief tech inspector, I became the chief race judge, which in the past been an honorary position. When I took over, I got things organized. I selected a group of ten men who had been around racing, either as drivers or workers, men who I felt would make good observers. Buddy Erlich had set up a phone network, with a phone on each corner and one at the start/finish line. With a judge and a phone on each corner, we developed a well-run system, and devised a list of all possible calls: spin, off course, fluid leak, balking, erratic driving, accident, etc.

The person at race central had a chart and would enter the various calls opposite the car numbers, according to a rigid system. For example, after two spins or similar calls, the starter waved a furled black flag – the driver knew what he had done wrong. One more similar call and the driver was black flagged, stopped and given a "talking-to" or was sent home, probably to be invited to the next contest board meeting.

I know in my heart that if this judging system had been in place a few years earlier, at least one of our former top drivers would still be alive.

I had a good group of judges. We looked quite professional, dressed in white pants and black & white striped referee shirts. We met at the conclusion of each day of racing and rehashed the day's events, over a few beers.

*   *   *   *

At one Paramount Ranch race, for reasons of safety, the pit entrance was changed, and it was explained to all of the drivers that in order to make a pit stop, for whatever reason, it was mandatory to use a special lane that began in the last turn.

During the main event, Ken Miles, who had a huge lead, bypassed the new entrance, stopped along the course in front of the pits, and his crewman handed him a cup of water. He rejoined the race, still in first place, and later threw the empty cup overboard.

Well!! One of my judges observed this and called for immediate disqualification. I concurred, but Joe Weissman, the race chairman, overrode our call, whereupon my judge threatened to quit his post. (I convinced him to stay.) Ken won the race and accepted the large trophy. But, at our post-race meeting, we judges voted unanimously to disqual-

ify Ken and later the contest board later backed us up. Ken, who was on the contest board, merely laughed; he had proved his point (he had the fastest car) and didn't care about the trophy.

Ken and I *still* remained good friends!

*　　*　　*　　*

In spite of my many enjoyable experiences, there were, unfortunately, some depressing times.

For example, in 1957, during the first race held at the new Riverside track, John Lawrence hit the bank on turn six. His MGA did a slow roll, and John's head was trapped under the rear deck. John died that night in the hospital. I was standing directly across the track and captured the incident on 16-mm film. I showed this to the Contest Board, and this helped convince them we should mandate roll bars, as a simple roll bar would have saved John's life.

From that point on, the Cal Club mandated roll bars. At first, there were no specifications given and some of the newly installed roll bars were probably worse than nothing. Some were made of exhaust tubing, and some left room for the driver's head to be trapped in case of a roll over. At least I was somewhat responsible for getting the ball rolling and undoubtedly saving some lives.

One of the potentially worst accidents occurred at a Pomona race. My wife, Joan, along with Dottie Dickinson and Louise Barlow, did the timing and scoring. As they had to be located at the start/finish line, I worried about their safety and insisted they be placed in an elevated position. To comply with my demands, a flatbed trailer was placed at the start/finish area for them to work on in relative safety.

During the main event, I was judging on turn three when the race was red-flagged. I knew there had been an accident at the start/finish line, so I hopped on my motorbke and sped back to the scene. As I approached the start/finish area, I couldn't believe the sight that met my eyes.

While exiting the last turn, Max Balchowsky's car blew its engine and deposited all of the oil on the track. A few cars got through safely, but Bruce Kessler, driving the Sadler Special, may have been looking for a pit signal and didn't see the oil. He spun at high speed and headed directly for the official area at the start/finish line. I don't know what happened first, but part of the car body hit the race chairman, Joe Weissman, and knocked him into the scaffolding, severely damaging his face. Whatever Kessler hit, he was projected out of the car and landed on a man standing at the edge of the track. Both were hurt, but not critically. The car then struck Virginia Beers (wife of Dwight Beers, one of my race judges), severing her leg. The Sadler finally came to rest after stacking up several cars, including one of the ambulances and J. C. Agajanian's Cadillac.

My first concern was about Joan. In all of the confusion, I asked Dan Dickinson about her. He didn't know what to say. He thought I said, Joe, not Joan. Joe was already on his way to the hospital, with Joan in attendance. She was a close friend of his and also a trained nurse. Joe later credited her for saving his life.

As soon as I could leave the track, I went to the hospital and was greatly relieved to find that Joan was not hurt.

Bruce spent a few days in the hospital, as did Joe, who had his face reconstructed. Both made complete recoveries.

On a cheerier note, I crewed for Ken Miles for nine months when he was racing his first MG Special, R-1. I had nothing to do with the car but did his timing, scoring, strategy and signaling.

In 1953, during a very hot July race at the Chino Airport, Ken had, as usual, won the under 1500cc race and was therefore allowed to compete in the main event (for large engine cars), starting at the back. I had always wondered just how much Ken relied on my signals to him. Well, I was about to find out.

Ken and I worked out strategy for the big race. He told me who he expected to beat and whom he probably couldn't. As the race progressed, Ken was far up in the field, 3rd or 4th overall. I had him on "hold" as I thought that was the best we could do. For two laps he came by pointing to the front of his car. I couldn't see anything wrong, even with binoculars. Someone said, "maybe he wants to pass the Jaguar Special" he was following. Next time around, I gave Ken the "faster" signal. Sure enough, he immediately went around the Jag and gained a position.

Another time, at Palm Springs, I had Ken on "hold" for several laps while he was following a slower car. I knew the gas tank was coming adrift on the car in front and it was about to be black-flagged. Ken trusted me and obeyed my signals to him.

I realized that Ken, being an unusually intelligent driver, knew we in the pits might have knowledge unavailable to him while he was driving.

So, races are won or lost through a combination of strategy, skill and luck,

* * * *

When I began officiating, I acquired an ex-British collapsible paratroop bike, which I used to get around to the various turns.

50

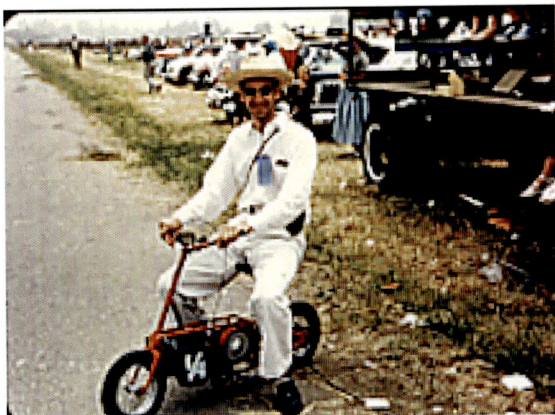

"Evil Knievel" Moss on his high-powered scooter!

It wasn't long before I graduated to a Triumph motorcycle. This enabled me to get to choice spots and exercise my various cameras. I started with 35mm, graduated to a 2¼ Mamiyaflex, and also used a 16mm Bolex movie camera. Some of my shots proved invaluable when bringing a driver before the contest board.

I was able to clip my headset to the communication line wherever I happened to be, thereby staying in touch with the other judges and race central.

Speaking of communication, the United States Auto Club (USAC), the sanctioning body of open-wheel racing, scheduled a stock car race at Paramount Ranch. This was to be their first venture on a non-oval, or road course.

We offered to provide them with judges, corner workers and communication. They wanted no help at all. So, early in the morning on the day of their race, a few of us wormed our way in and hooked our headsets to the underground communication lines we had installed a few years before. We proceeded to enjoy the race, keeping each other informed about what was happening at each turn.

After several laps, USAC realized they had not the slightest clue what was happening out of sight of the start/finish line. Pretty soon we were running their race, informing them of a car spilling fuel, dragging something, or of an accident.

*   *   *   *

Just so you don't have the idea that we always took our racing seriously, I offer this account from a memorable race in the San Diego area. In addition to fun and games at the motel swimming pool (Ken Miles getting tossed in and Richie Ginther almost riding his motor scooter into the pool), we organized the first, last, and only race for pit bikes.

Twelve intrepid riders showed up for the start. Richie borrowed a bike, Len Ridder wore John Porter's unique driving suit, and I borrowed Ken Miles green crash hat. The race lasted for one lap, which probably took up the whole lunch hour. Richie's bike broke down and he came across the finish line riding on the back of Cy Yedor's motorcycle, holding the scooter on his lap. I don't remember who won, but a good time was had by all!

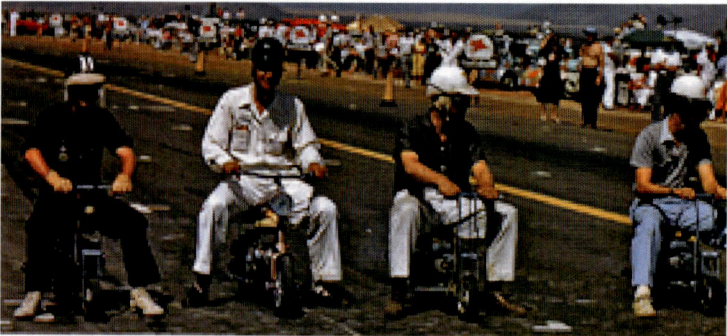

Yours truly second from the left wearing Ken Miles' green crash hat.

Richie Ginther on the left, next to Len Ridder.

We had some wild parties after the Saturday races. But, contrary to popular belief, I did NOT ride a motorcycle into the swimming pool at the Santa Barbara Miramar hotel. Here's what really happened.

After dinner, I attempted to ride a more than slightly inebriated Cy Yedor on the handlebars of the bellboy's bicycle to go get his motorcycle. We promptly crashed in the bushes outside the dining room windows, to the amusement of all inside. On the way back to join the party, with Cy driving the motorcycle and me as passenger, we circled the swimming pool. I almost dumped us both into the pool, but thought better of it, as I knew I would end up cleaning the Triumph!

That was the night of the Big Bongo Party in Ruth Levy's room.

But that's another story...

* * * *

During the time I was involved with road racing in the 1950s and early sixties, I had the opportunity to take a great many photographs, both stills and movies.

In 2006, I transferred these films into my Mac computer. I then edited and narrated them, and, with background music, ended up with a very nice set of four DVDs containing over four hours of racing pictures. For more information, go to: www.racermoss.com

I am deeply indebted to Peter Egan, one of the most popular and widely read American authors of automotive and motorcycle articles. Peter's monthly *Road & Track* column, "Side Glances", in December 2006, featured the DVD set and me. This led to an avalanche of orders.

In December 2007, the Southern California chapter of the Society of Automotive Historians honored me with the James Valentine award, given for the first time in the electronic media category. Apparently, they were impressed by my DVDs!

13 Moss's Hoss's

Not long after moving to Santa Barbara in 1963, I developed an interest in horses, which came as a big surprise to me. I found horses challenging – something new to learn about, and, perhaps more importantly, they opened a whole new world to me – a world not associated with *cars!* My involvement with cars (racing, clubs, rallying and organizing events) was because of my profound enthusiasm and interest in such activities. However, I had heard occasional comments such as, "He's doing that (whatever) for *business* reasons." But since I had nothing to sell the horsie set, my involvement with horses was not suspect.

First thing, I bought a well-used, high-mileage palomino steed, complete with bridle and saddle, for two hundred bucks. Pretty cheap, or so I thought. Then I found I had to pay for stabling, feeding, shoeing, and veterinary care for the animal. Next, I purchased a horse trailer and discovered it required something to *pull* it. So, I bought an old, well-used, Ford pickup truck. (After repainting the trailer, I had neatly lettered on each side, "Moss's Hoss's").

I made several new horse friends (people, not animals) and was invited on a weekend trail ride. The Santa Barbara Trail Riders is a group of would-be cowboys who ride four times a year on different ranches. My first ride was on a ranch bordering the Pacific Ocean. It was quite an experience: riding, drinking and eating, with a bunch of guys. They have a portable, always open bar, the food is catered and plentiful, and the riding both days enjoyable.

After joining the SBTR and participating for a few years, I became acquainted with competitive trail riding. What, you are wondering, is a competitive trail ride? Allow me to explain.

There is a "time/speed/distance" similarity between a competitive trail ride and a sports car rally, in that each horse and rider must negotiate a mapped and marked course. Rides of thirty-five to forty miles in 6-1/2 to 7 hours on each of two days were common. The horses are judged by a team of veterinarians, as to soundness, condition and way-of-going. Separate awards are given for the rider's horsemanship. The events I entered took place in California, Arizona and Colorado and were sanctioned by the North American Trail Ride Conference (NATRC).

In 1964, I acquired a very tall quarter horse named Baron and entered my first competitive ride in Santa Barbara. I was immediately hooked; here was something more challenging than just trail riding. I spent many hours in the saddle conditioning Baron and myself. I had to learn how to properly feed and care for a horse under stressful conditions. These rides took me into areas and on ranches I would never have known, otherwise.

After a short while, I began managing competitive rides in the Santa Barbara area, first in the Santa Ynez wilderness. This was a time-consuming process. First, permission had to be obtained from the head ranger. Then all trails were pre-ridden and mapped, with mileages determined. A large enough area had to be secured to allow camping for thirty to forty people, places to tie the horses, and space to park all of the "rigs" (trailers, trucks and campers). Veterinarians and horsemanship judges had to be hired. The local Jeep club volunteered to transport the judges and P&R teams during both days of the ride. (P&R teams are volunteers who are stationed at the top of steep climbs to take the pulse and respiration of each incoming horse, note the readings, and do a re-check a few minutes later. The rate of recovery helps determine the

condition of each horse.) The riders were divided into three groups: heavyweight, lightweight and junior

After putting on these spring rides for a few years, I obtained permission from several landowners to put on a fall ride in the Santa Ynez Mountains. This included the Tip Top Ranch, which was owned by Raymond Cornelius. The ranch is located atop the Santa Ynez mountain range, at the top of Refugio (the Refuge) Road. Raymond was kind enough to drive me around the area and show me many little-known sites, such as caves with old Indian petroglyphs and the site where a Canadian Air Force airplane crashed fatally during World War II.

I spent some time in the adobe house Raymond used as a lodge. It was a small house, built in 1872. A small pond sat near the house. I put on three or four competitive rides in this location prior to the 688-acre property being sold to Governor Ronald Reagan in 1974. During Reagan's presidency, this was the only residence he owned.

When Reagan moved in, my riding days in that area came to an end. I contemplated writing a letter to him, offering to bring my horse up and show him the trails and "secret" places on his new property, as Raymond Cornelius had passed away and there were probably very few people who knew the area as well as I. This letter remained unwritten, as I thought it would probably be ignored and I might be susceptible to an FBI or CIA investigation! From what I learned of President Reagan after his death, I was probably wrong and he might have welcomed me. Oh well!

My career in competitive trail riding lasted quite a few years. I competed in over seventy events, served on the board of the North American Trail Ride Conference for several years, and as president for two years. The NATRC is still going strong – stronger than ever – and provides scholarships to needy children. The NATRC does not stage

rides, but functions as a sanctioning body, providing judges and stewards, plus writing rule books and manuals.

During my time with horses I had some wonderful experiences on trail rides, in parades and, yes, in one horse show. I was coerced into entering a big Arabian Horse Show on my Arabian, Fersann, and rode in full Arab costume (beard, cape, and all the trappings), perched high on an old cavalry saddle. When it came time for the high-speed gallop around the ring, I was, quite frankly, *terrified*, as I wasn't sure I could ever stop spirited Fersann. When the command came to stop, I pulled frantically on the reins and finally Fersann decided to STOP. Quickly and firmly. I could feel the whole thing (Moss, saddle, costume, false beard and all) starting to topple. Luckily, I regained my balance and did not land in a colorful heap in the arena in front of a large audience. That was my last horse show!

Sahib Moss on Fersann.

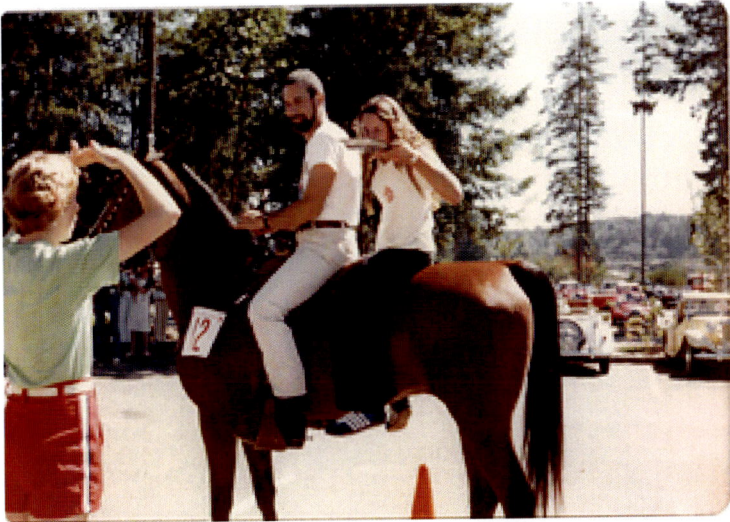

An unusual photograph, to say the least! In 1977, Nancy and I were planning to attend the MG meet in Olympia, Washington. At the last minute, I decided to take our camper and two horses, instead of the MG. We had a pleasant trip up the coast, camping and riding along the way, even galloping on the Oregon Dunes.

At the MG Gathering, I entered my horse, Shah Jahn, in the funkhana, with Peggy Thelander as my co-driver. We went through the whole course, including the backing-up part, with Peggy trying not to spill water from the platter. Jahn sported an MG radiator cap and badge on top of his bridle. This was the first time Jahn had ever packed double and he did an admirable job of it. (We didn't win the event!)

During my "horsie" years, I had some memorable experiences. In 1965 I was instrumental in forming a horse club in Santa Barbara. This club, The Los Padres Riders club is still going strong.

Occasionally, I would take a few provisions for myself and my horse and journey into the backcountry; just the two of us to enjoy nature and camp out for a few nights. On two occasions, six other men and I packed into the wilderness area for three days and nights, packing all our food on a mule. I miss those days, but have fond memories.

Traversing Hurricane Deck in the Santa Barbara Wilderness.

I had a succession of horses: quarter horses and Arabians. My last horse was Shah Jahn, a 3/4 Arabian (the remaining ¼ must have been Ferrari!) We got off to a poor start, and when I got out of the hospital it took us some time to get re-acquainted. When we finally did, Jahn turned out to be the best horse I ever had. Unfortunately, around 1994, he developed some serious ailments and had to be put down. I gave up riding after that.

As an adjunct to my horse experiences, my two daughters, Cindy and Juli, were also involved with the beasts. I was proud to see them garner numerous, beautiful awards during the years they competed in horse shows, stadium jumping and competitive trail riding.

14 The Saga of Baron Moss

Shortly after Joan and I got settled in Santa Barbara, we purchased a two-acre parcel of land in the foothills and began planning a house. With the help of a friend, I started constructing a stable on the property. I took off work a few hours each afternoon to work on it, and in order to stay in contact with Moss Motors, I had a telephone installed at the site. As my horse's name was Baron, I decided to register the phone in the name of Baron Moss. Then the fun began!

Telephone solicitors were constantly calling, asking to speak with Baron Moss. He received a camera for a gift, and someone attempted to serve him with a subpoena! This made the front page of the local newspaper several times. These articles came to the attention of the telephone company and they sent a reporter and photographer from Santa Monica to interview us. The resulting article appeared in the phone company's newsletters nationwide. It then appeared worldwide in Ripley's "Believe it or Not."

When several articles, with Baron's phone number, appeared in the local paper, I started getting calls from all sorts of people who wanted to talk with him. Kids would call, asking when they could come and ride Baron, and one day a woman called to sell something to Baron Moss. After considerable discussion, I finally said the reason he could not come to the phone was because he was a horse. She said, "Young man, you're putting me on. Let me speak with your *mother.*"

We kept this phone listing after we moved into our newly built home. It had all the advantages of an unlisted number without having to pay a monthly fee for one.

In 1971, Nancy, my second wife, and I built a new house and listed the phone in my current horse's name, Shah Jahn (King John in Arabic). It remained like that for several years until I concocted the name Henrietta Glockenspiel and listed the phone under that name.

While the phone was listed under my horse's name, a friend who had recently moved to a small town in Colorado, thought this was rather funny, so he listed his phone under his dog's name, Trina. A friend of his called me one day, asking if I knew how to contact Dave. I told him to ask information for Trina Puppy's number. I knew he thought I was putting him on, but he called back a few minutes later, laughing. Seems he called information and the gal told him, "Yes, I have a listing for Miss Puppy!"

After my phone had been listed in Henrietta Glockenspiel's name, I went to the local telephone company office to conduct some business. The tall, prim, lady behind the counter looked up from her computer, and asked, "Did your father *invent* the glockenspiel?"

I replied, "No, Ma'am, that was my grandfather."

After a pause, "Do you *play* the glockenspiel?"

I replied, "No Ma'am; I play the harmonica."

A bit later, "Why *don't* you play the glockenspiel?"

"Because I can't carry it on my bicycle."

"Oh."

I am sure at dinner that night Ms. Prim announced to her family, "Guess who *I* met today?"

*   *   *   *

By the way, Baron never did manage to get any good pictures with his free camera.

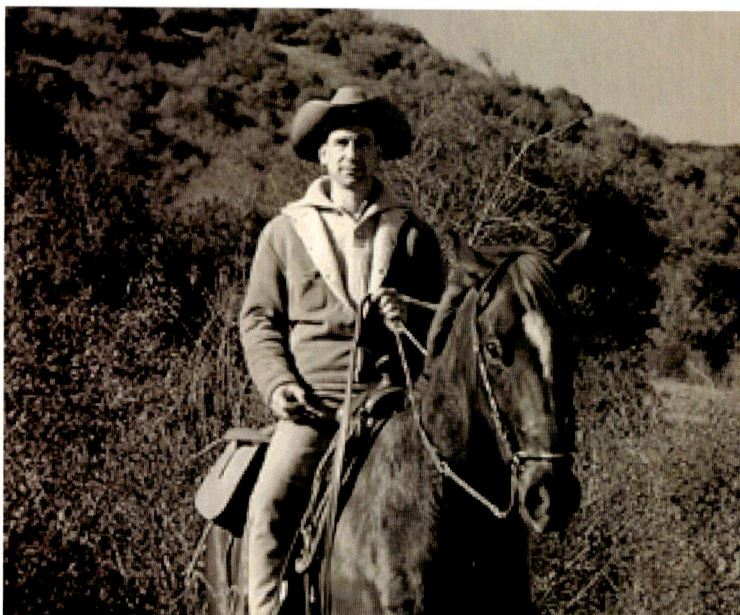

*Baron (registered name: Baronet) was a 6-year-old quarter horse,
16 ¾ hands tall. I was much younger then!*

15 Juan de Anza Moss

One of the highlights of my life occurred in 1976, the bicentennial year of our country. In that year, while great celebrations were taking place back East, a significant event was occurring out West.

In the year 1774, a Spaniard, Juan de Anza, urged the Viceroy of Mexico to authorize an expedition from Sonora, Mexico, to Monterey, California, for the purpose of establishing a shorter and safer route than existing ones. He led a band of thirty-three soldiers, who survived Apache raids and a near disaster in the desert, all the way to Monterey.

As a result of this successful expedition, late in 1775 de Anza led a group of 242 people, including soldiers, their wives and children, three missionaries and four civilian settlers from Tubac, Mexico, to Monterey, California. They brought no wagons, but did have 695 horses and 355 head of cattle. One mother died in childbirth, but her baby survived, as did seven others born along the way.

Their route went from Horcasitas, in Senora, Mexico, through Nogales, Tucson, Casa Grande, Yuma, Borrego Springs, Riverside, Santa Barbara and Lompoc to Monterey, a distance of about 1600 miles. The trek took about four months. Later, part of the group went on to San Francisco. The purpose of this expedition was to colonize California, and had nothing to do with establishing missions. That came later with Father Junipero Serra.

So, in 1976, several hundred intrepid, West Coast folks participated in a reenactment of the original de Anza trek. Two diaries had been kept on the original trek, one by de Anza himself and the other by Father Pedro Font, the expedition's chaplain. Thanks to this valuable information, an accurate reenactment was made possible, following the

exact route, and stopping or camping in many of the original locations.

In 1975, I was asked to portray de Anza for the entire Santa Barbara County segment of the reenactment. This involved growing a beard (which I kept for ten years), donning a period costume (complete with sword and cape), and leading the trek for one week across the county. At first, I thought this was a pretty ridiculous assignment, but the closer we got to the actual reenactment, the more I realized what an honor it was to portray a famous person in California history. When I took charge the first day, it was a real challenge to get the group underway. Once the large contingent got moving, the trek proved to be one of excitement and ceremony. On two occasions, the Highway Patrol blocked Highway 101 for us to traverse. We also stopped at several schools where the children, who had been studying de Anza, asked many questions, which, thankfully, I was prepared to answer. In addition to those of us mounted on horses (and one mule), there were foot soldiers and their "wives," as well as a few "Indian guides." Altogether, quite a procession, which created quite a stir along the route.

On my first day as de Anza, I was riding next to a donkey ridden by a man dressed as, and representing, Father Font, the priest who was on the original 1776 trek. Assuming he was just another one of us in costume, I started calling him "Dad.' Imagine my embarrassment when I learned he was actually the local Catholic Priest! He was very good natured and we became friends.

* * * *

Juan de Anza Moss & Shah Jahn.

On our first day in Santa Barbara, I led the large group across the main highway and onto the beach, where a celebration was held, with de Anza meeting the Chumash Indians (who came ashore in their large, newly-constructed replica "canoe"). We exchanged beads for fish and enjoyed a shark barbecue, courtesy of the local Chumash Tribe. The mayor and other dignitaries were there, as were television crews. I was given the honor of a ride in the sacred Chumash canoe. When we got beyond the breakers, the boat started rocking, and I heard a voice from the back of the boat say, "White man bring wallet?"

The mayor introducing Juan de Anza (Moss).

As part of the ceremony, I was supposed to exchange beads with the Indian Chief for a fish he just caught. I was totally unaware that the museum curator was afraid that if the sacred beads from the museum were handed to the Chief, he would not return them. When the Chief handed me the fish, he whispered to me, "Where beads?" Taken by surprise, all I could think to say was, "Beads on back-order!"

While no one person or horse made the entire reenactment trek, George Cardinet (remember the Cardinet Candy Company – makers of the Uno Bar?) had a replica of a *mochila* made. Spanish for "knapsack," the mochila was placed over the saddle and was used to carry maps, important documents and mail. Pony Express riders used it because it could be quickly transferred to a fresh horse. This mochila was transferred to each new "de Anza" along the way.

After a fantastic week of riding, camping, huge nightly barbeques, and making lasting friendships, my week of portraying Juan de Anza, sadly came to an end. Four of us, (including my wife, Nancy (who did all of the preliminary route and trail scouting), and Vie and George Obern (who were the prime instigators and organizers of the Santa Barbara segment), went home, cleaned ourselves, our horses and tack and rejoined the trek at Camp Roberts,

riding all the way into Monterey, where celebrations, a parade, and banquet were held. A perfect ending to a wonderful, once-in-a lifetime, experience.

I led the group many miles along Santa Barbara's beaches.

*   *   *   *

Some of my favorite recollections are:

— Finishing the Santa Barbara County segment in Guadalupe, the farthest-west city in the county, and having lunch at the Far Western Tavern.

— Finding my picture in local newspapers. After turning over the mochila to the new de Anza, shortly before our early morning departure from Vandenberg Air Base, rain began falling. Without meaning to be funny, but wanting to remain dry, I removed my small, collapsible umbrella from behind my saddle and opened it up. So, guess who had his picture on the front page of the local newspapers? Not the new de Anza!

— Having the Highway Patrol stop traffic and lead us across busy Highway 101. We then had our lunch stop in Gaviota State Park, where horses are normally not allowed. During lunch, while we were all gathered under a big oak tree, Vie Obern read us a passage from Father Font's diary, in which he described the 1776 trek and how they camped in the same spot *under the same tree!*

— The daily problem of getting our rigs from the previous day's camp to the next night's camp. It somehow always worked out!

— Meeting several ancestors of the participants who had been on the original expedition, two-hundred years ago.

— The barbecues and parties during and after the reenactment.

— Riding as de Anza, along with a group of reenactment participants, in the annual Santa Barbara Fiesta Parade – for several years following the reenactment.

Recognize this location? It's the Laguna Seca racetrack.

Now, back to car stuff.

16   Bicentennial Rally

To help celebrate our Bicentennial Year, the New England MG-T Register organized a week-long rally through the thirteen original colonies. British Leyland, makers of MG, sponsored the event and was kind enough to donate a very special MGB (the one-millionth produced) as first prize.

A total of 37 MGs were entered in the rally, which began in Savannah, Georgia, on Monday, July 26, 1976, and finished in Philadelphia the following Saturday. The main object of this rally was to go from start to finish each day with the least mileage. There were a few checkpoints along the way, to keep the teams honest. Additionally, there were a few special tests during the week: a tire changing contest, a spark plug changing contest, an economy run and a TSD (time, speed, distance) leg.

A few months prior to the event, I received a phone call from my good friend, the late Lou Zuger, inviting me to navigate for him in his MG TC. After eagerly accepting Lou's invitation, I made arrangements to fly to Savannah the day prior to the start. I had no sooner arrived than I was asked to examine all of the cars to make sure they were roadworthy, safe and in complience with the Highway Code and rally rules. All of the cars passed 100% with the exception of – you guessed it – Lou's TC! While working on the car all afternoon in the sweltering heat and humidity, I couldn't help wondering if this wasn't, perhaps, why Lou invited me. Nah!!

A few weeks before I was to depart for Savannah, I received a phone call from someone at British Leyland, wanting to know my sizes: hat, shirt, pants, etc. At first I was sure this was a joke, but no – British Leyland wanted one team dressed in period colonial costumes, and

Lou and I were to be the lucky ones. We were given a schedule telling us when and where to don these outfits: at the start, several stops along the way, and at the finish, where they had camera crews waiting for us. Naturally, we all had plenty of laughs over this garb – like when changing into our costumes at a truck stop, Lou said, "Martha, your stockings are crooked!"

George and Martha.

While a few diehard entrants went for the big prize, most of us went just to have a good time. And we did! Lou and I did not take the whole thing seriously, and, even with all my past rally experience, I completely blew the time/speed/distance leg. In spite of this goof and thanks to a poor scoring system, Lou and I still placed third overall. Just as well we didn't win. How would we have divided the first place prize?

17 GoF, HCT, SCC, & RRR

In 1964, two MG enthusiasts from New England, Frank Churchill and Dick Knudson, got together and formed a register of T-Series MG owners. When I learned about this, I mentioned it in my MG catalog, which gave a big boost to the project. The Register is still going strong, having had a worldwide membership of 15,000 a few years ago.

In 1965, the Register organized the first "Gathering of the Faithful" (GoF). You have to be pretty faithful to drive an old MG to distant events! The GoFs have continued without interruption ever since, usually with a spring and fall event each year. Between 1965 and 2007, the New England MG-T Register has hosted over 81 "Gatherings."

A typical GoF takes place over four days and consists of several events: a rally/tour, a "funkhana" (driving skill events), an evening auction of MG-related items, and a display of all the cars, with entrants voting for their favorite car in each class. The last evening, an awards banquet is enjoyed, and the finale is a farewell breakfast.

The first Gathering I attended was at Mt. Snow, Vermont, in 1968. In 1972, I met with a group of fellow Californians and we decided to put on a GoF on the West Coast. After deciding on Santa Barbara as an ideal location for our first effort, we each kicked in fifty dollars to get the ball rolling.

The first GoF-West was held at the Miramar Hotel in October 1973, and proved to be a success. This led to the formation of a GoF-West Steering Committee composed of four members. I felt honored to be selected to serve on this committee, and I served for many years. The purpose of this committee was, and still is, to provide guidelines for future gatherings and to select and approve clubs to put on future events.

There has been an annual GoF-West each year since 1973. They have been held in all the western states and Canada, following the format just described.

In 1976, the Santa Barbara MG Club hosted a "Mini GoF," at Morro Bay. As the event included a tour of Hearst Castle, it was called "HCT" (Hearst Castle Tour). I took over the chairmanship of this event and it was held there until 1983, at which time the host hotel folded its tent and faded away into the night, and another venue could not be found.

HCT was always a fun, low-key event and was sorely missed by the past attendees. In 2001, I was prevailed upon to stage an "HCT revival." By then, I was living in Sedona, Arizona – what better place to hold this event?

I selected a suitable hotel, sent out invitations, and began the time-consuming task of laying out a rally, organizing the funkhana events, and undertaking tasks of designing a logo, and of printing all the necessary forms, name tags, ballots, programs, etc. (Thank heavens for my computer, a Mac of course.) For awards, I collected an assortment of flat, red rocks, which abound in Sedona, cleaned each one and affixed plaques denoting what the award was for. Each one was set on an easel; they looked great and were well received by the winners.

The first HCT (High Country Tour), in 2002, was limited to thirty-six cars/couples and it went off with nary a hitch. Even the weather cooperated. It rained the night prior to the rally, but the day dawned bright and beautiful. In spite of the work involved, I thoroughly enjoyed the fruits of my efforts. Seeing so many friends enjoying the three days of HCT made all the work worthwhile.

Whilst these events are limited to MG owners, I realized there are times when a few true-blue MG enthusiasts are unable to bring their MGs to an event. I therefore created a class for "the best MG in disguise." Some owners got very creative, adorning their non-MGs with MG logos, etc.

So anyway, being a glutton for punishment, I decided to organize another HCT again in 2004 – same hotel, same format, different rally, some new faces. This, also, was a smashing success. And, wouldn't you know, I did it again in 2006. This was the last time, for sure! (Now I am planning a 2009 HCP – High Country Party!)

TCs lined up for the car display. HCT, 2002.

*   *   *   *   *

Upon settling in Sedona in 1997, I joined the Sedona Car Club, an active club with about sixty-five family memberships. I was asked to serve on the executive board in the capacity of tour chairman. I also served as president in 2004 and 2005. As tour chairman, I organized many events, ranging from short, one-day events (such as rallies, garage tours, garage sales, etc.) to three and five-day tours. The latter included visiting Indian ruins and villages with a

professor from the University of Northern Arizona as our guide, and tours through Utah's National Parks: Bryce, Zion, Capitol Reef and Arches. We also had tours of the Ford Proving Grounds, old Route 66, the local cement plant, and Kartchner Caverns.

Organizing these events is enjoyable to me, and the club members who attend seem to enjoy them, as well. I will be the tour chairman again in 2008.

Recently, I joined the Red Rock Racers, a local non-club composed of twelve guys who are all actively engaged in vintage racing – not real early vintage cars, but an assortment of Porsches, Alfa Romeos, a pair of Lotuses (Loti?), an Elva, etc. We meet for lunch weekly and do lots of bench racing. Shades of the Moss Motors Luncheon & Bench Racing Society!

Last, but not least, is the Fabulous Fifties, another non-club composed of those who were racing in the 1950s, or wish they had been. There are no meetings, but we have several get-togethers each year and there's an occasional newsletter and annual banquet at the Peterson Museum.

*　　*　　*　　*

I have been honored through the years by being presented with several awards for helping to organize events and for doing my part in keeping several thousand old MGs running and on the road. Among these are the Founders Award, presented by the New England MG-T Register in 1968, and the Mac Spears Founders Award, presented by the North American MGA Register, "In recognition of significant contributions to NAMGAR and/or the preservation of the MGA."

These and similar awards mean the world to me, and have helped me to see how worthwhile my contributions have been to others.

18 Motorcycle Mania

All through my high school years I had a burning desire to own a motorcycle. My parents, being of sound mind, would hear nothing about this and forbade me from even thinking seriously about acquiring such a noisy and dangerous contraption. I nearly had them convinced when, while driving my car, I glanced down at a Harley-Davidson brochure, drifted to the right and collided with a parked car. While no serious damage occurred to either vehicle, this ended any further discussion about motorcycles.

During my college days, I became friendly with a fellow-student who owned a Harley-Davidson. It was a rather clapped out, war surplus, 80 cubic-inch bike with a reverse gear, as it had been fitted with a sidecar during the war. The owner went away for summer break and left the bike with me for safekeeping. The rear tire was bald, so he knew I would not be riding it very much. But I learned to ride and even do a few stunts – without ever "dropping" the machine.

My interest continued, and, after being married to Joan for a few years, I broached the subject of purchasing a motorbike. Joan threatened to leave me if I did such a crazy thing. I did, but luckily, she didn't! I bought a nearly new Triumph Tiger Cub and began using it in my duties as chief race judge at the Cal Club sports car races. Between races I would ride around to check with my judges, and take them their lunches at noon. This also enabled me to get to ideal spots for picture taking.

I established a contact enabling me to purchase a new, current-model Triumph every October when the new models came out. My cost was about half of the retail price. So, I would purchase a new 650cc Triumph, ride it

a few years, then sell it and purchase a new one. This continued until I moved to Santa Barbara in 1963. I sold my last Triumph at that time and went bikeless for several years, until I purchased a new Honda 350. This bike fit in with my competitive trail riding. I was able to use it for checking dirt roads and unrestricted trails, and for tying trail-marker ribbons prior to a weekend competitive ride.

Following the Honda, I had a succession of Japanese sport bikes: a Honda 400-4, a Kawasaki GPZ550, a GPZ750, and my favorite, a Yamaha RZ350, (a water-cooled two-stroke screamer). I rode sport bikes exclusively, rather than big, heavy touring machines, as I found the former to be light, easy to handle and extremely comfortable on long, cross-country trips. Also, I could sneak them into motel rooms for the night, keeping them warm, dry and safe from theft.

Arguably, the finest classic British motorcycle is the Vincent Black Shadow. In the 1950s, these were the fastest production vehicles made, motorcycle or car. I owned two of these magnificent machines. The first one, I purchased in 1954, from a customer who had completely dismantled the very complex machine. I managed to assemble it, but as it took shape and I realized what a monster I was creating, I went out and bought a Triumph Tiger Cub to ride. I sold the Vincent after it was together and running.

The totally dismantled Vincent.

My second Vincent Black Shadow.

In 1983, I purchased my second Vincent Black Shadow. I rebuilt the entire engine and, once I solved the problem of it not starting when hot, I had a wonderful, reliable and beautiful machine that attracted attention wherever I rode it. I made several annual trips to Laguna Seca for the July motorcycle-race weekend. After several years of proud ownership, and prior to my 1997 move from Santa Barbara to Sedona, I, regrettably, sold the Vincent. By the way, Jay Leno owns and rides one of the finest Black Shadows I have ever seen.

I sold my Yamaha a few years ago and am no longer riding. One reason is that my replacement knee doesn't bend far enough to allow me to put my left foot on the peg or to work the gearshift, and I'll be damned if I'll buy a Harley, with its feet-forward position! Another reason is Sedona traffic – between the old folks and tourists, riding a motorcycle in this town could be hazardous to my health.

I just finished restoring this 1967 Triumph 650cc Trophy.

The absolute highlight of my motorcycle-mania days came in June of 1985, when I spent a week on the Isle of Man. Located across the Irish Sea, 60 miles from England, this small, 227-square-mile island, is the scene for the annual week of motorcycle activities. It is also where the breed of tailless Manx cats originated. Ever since I was a kid, I yearned to go there and witness an exciting week of motorcycle racing.

Two friends from Santa Barbara (Nels Miller and David Green) and I thoroughly enjoyed the week of motorcycle mania. On Monday, Wednesday and Friday we watched high-speed races around the 37¾-mile circuit. Alternate days offered all sorts of other activities: one-make gatherings, tours, demonstrations, observed trials, etc. Each evening there were also many activities: more trials, visiting with bikers from all over the world, wet T-shirt contests, and, you name it!

We had taken my rental car over on the ferry and were able to drive on interior roads to various spots on the long course. Thanks to Debbie Earle of General Racing, I had press credentials and was able to get into choice spots with my video camera.

We stayed in a small hotel/bed & breakfast in Douglas. Every morning the residents, all motorcycle enthusiasts, converged in the dining hall– always for the same English breakfast: two fried eggs, tomatoes, bacon and toast. One morning I sat down, still half asleep, and when my plate was placed before me, I tried cutting into the eggs – with no success, and said, to no one in particular, "these damn things are like rubber!" Everyone broke into laughter. My friend, Nels, had purchased two very real-looking *rubber* eggs and had tipped the kitchen staff to serve them to me. Everyone was wise to the joke, but kept perfectly quiet.

Nels had a rather diabolical sense of humor. Before leaving for England, and the Isle of Man, he had an upholsterer make fifty flexible furry feline fanny tails. He felt sorry for all the poor Manx kitties having to go through life with no tails. He gave his furry tails to some of the local inhabitants and one to Mick Grant, the top British trials rider.

I had one hanging out of my camera bag and several people wanted to know if I had a cat in there. Of course, we visited the Manx cattery and there Nels handed his little tails out freely.

For the benefit of those of you who were around sports car racing in the 1950s, Nels was the son of Dusty Miller, who raced a Maserati and later bought and raced the ex-Ken Miles R-1 MG. Nels inherited and restored the MG and raced it at Monterey in 1979. He passed away in 1991.

19 Observed Trials

What is an Observed Trial? Well, for starters, an observed trial has absolutely nothing to do with lawyers, judges, juries, lawsuits or courtrooms.

In England, motorcycles have always been a popular form of transportation and sport, and this naturally led to various forms of two-wheeled competition. A popular sport developed, requiring the rider to negotiate a difficult section of terrain without putting a foot down or falling. This became known as an "observed trial."

In modern-day trials there will be a loop – a circuit usually one or two miles in length. Along this loop there will be sections, usually about ten in number. The riders navigate the loop, stopping at each section. The section is marked out with ribbon or chalk and once the riders enter the section, they try to negotiate the section without falling over or allowing either foot to touch the ground. The section may contain rocks, boulders, hills and streams. The rider is observed by a "checker," an observer who deducts one point each time the rider "dabs," or touches the ground. After three dabs, the rider may still continue, dabbing if necessary, until he completes the section without falling or going out of bounds, thereby receiving the maximum of five points.

The motorcycles used in trials riding are a special breed. They are very light in weight, and the front wheel can be turned nearly ninety degrees in either direction. The seat is virtually nonexistent, as the rider stands on the pegs while competing, allowing the bike to move freely between his legs.

There is no time involved, either in riding the loop or sections. Each rider starts with a clean sheet and receives one point for each dab, or five for failing the section. The

object is to finish with a clean sheet. There are four classes, from beginner through novice to expert. The loop is ridden three or four times.

In the early 1980s, I became acquainted with this challenging sport, acquired a secondhand Spanish Bultaco (the leading bike at one time), and began practicing – practicing – practicing. The older one gets (and I was gettin' there), the more difficult it is to develop the balance required to ride very slowly, and to remain motionless for several seconds without "dabbing."

Finally, the day came when I felt confident enough to actually enter a trial, naturally in the beginner class. This was a difficult and challenging event, requiring riders to negotiate a long, arduous loop, four times. I started out doing quite well, with several "clean" sections, but after the third loop, I was tiring; so I quit during the final loop, disqualifying myself from the competition. I went home exhausted, but happy – satisfied and hooked on the sport.

The next day a very competitive acquaintance came up and asked me, "Didja win?"

I thought for a moment and answered, "Yes, I won. I rode up to my capabilities and had FUN!" He, I got the feeling, couldn't understand this.

For several years, I continued practicing and entering trials all over California, moving up a class, making new friends, crashing numerous times, and thoroughly enjoying the time spent.

The sport of trials riding has never been terribly popular in our country; but is really huge in England and on the Continent, where the top riders are as well known as Wilt Chamberlain or Tiger Woods in this country. The lack of popularity in this country can be attributed to the lack of speed and danger involved. The modern generation seems to need to go fast and skirt death!

So, now that you know all about observed trials, aren't you glad you purchased this book?

A section comprised of rocks and boulders.

Entering a pond. Note the ribbons marking the section.

A Parable

In 1979, shortly after I sold Moss Motors and retired, the new owner was desirous of purchasing several vintage Rolls Royce automobiles. As he knew I had knowledge of these classics, he sent me off to England with a large amount of cash – a sufficient amount to purchase several of these very expensive vehicles.

Upon debarking at Heathrow, I was approached by a well-dressed, middle-aged man who welcomed me to London and offered to buy me a drink. I accepted his kind offer, and after a few drinks, this nice man informed me that he was in a position to offer me an opportunity of making some quick cash.

I became aware that the drinks he was buying were much stronger than I was used to, and they were starting to give me a warm, fuzzy feeling.

I was surprised when the kind gentleman informed me that he was an agent for a Columbian drug cartel, but I trusted him, so gave him the large packet of cash I had in my briefcase. We arranged to meet the following morning, when he was to return my cash, along with a handsome profit. I was happily looking forward to being able to purchase an additional Rolls Royce with this sudden windfall. Won't Moss Motors be proud of me!

Unfortunately, I have no recollection of leaving the airport or checking into my hotel. However, I did have many very weird and wonderful dreams that night.

The following morning I went to the designated meeting place, but the kind gentleman was nowhere to be seen. I waited until late afternoon, yet he never showed up. Then, alarmed. I went to the local Scotland Yard office. When I told the lieutenant my story, and described the man, the officer laughed and put me down as just one more American who got duped by the scam – involving free drinks, laced with methamphetamine tablets.

Moral: A stoned Moss gathers no Rolls.

20 Historic Auto Racing

Most race fans know that the finest race course on the West Coast, if not in the entire country, used to be Pebble Beach. Held on the beautiful Seventeen Mile Drive, near Carmel, this tree-lined course hosted seven races from 1950 though 1956. Unfortunately, there were no further races held there after that time.

In 1957, a new course was developed at nearby Laguna Seca, on Fort Ord, an older Army base. Motor vehicles of many types race on this course: motorcycles, sports cars, Can-Am and Indy cars. In 1974, a gentleman by the name of Steven Earle had the brilliant idea of staging a race for historic sports cars, and doing it like in the good old days – just a bunch of enthusiasts enjoying racing, with no spectators, no prize money, no awards – just a weekend of good racing.

This event was so successful, it was run annually, and today is the premier event of its kind in the world. Each year a different marque (make of car) is honored, and cars are brought from all over the world. The 2008 event will be the 35th.

It turned out that Steve Earle was a neighbor of mine in Santa Barbara, and he visited me one day in 1975, to chat and look at some of my old racing pictures. When he described his upcoming race, I decided to enter. My MG TC had been on display in the Moss Motors showroom and hadn't been driven for some six years. I had planned to bring it out and prepare it for a trip to Bend, Oregon, (for the West Coast MG gathering). Now I had another reason to do so.

After removing the plate-glass window from the showroom, and destroying considerable planting, the TC finally emerged. I spent a week restoring it to operation, then Nancy and I packed a few belongings and tools and

set out for Monterey. I raced the car for three days, had no trouble, and drove it back home to Santa Barbara after the races. The next week, we set out for Bend, spending a day in Reno. Dean Batchelor, who was then employed at Bill Harrah's huge automobile museum, gave us a personal tour of the entire facility, including a nice lunch in the cafeteria.

Departing from Reno, we enjoyed a trouble-free trip to Bend, where we participated in the various activities at the MG meet. Following the meet, we drove west to the Pacific Ocean, turned south and had a lovely, but very cold trip down the Coast Route (infamous Highway 1) to Santa Barbara.

I entered the TC in the Monterey Historic races for the next eleven years, and also competed at Sears Point, Buttonwillow and Palm Springs in the TC, as well as several other cars.

From 1986 through 1990, I competed with the ex-von Neumann, MG TD Special. (Chapter 21)

Al at speed in Old Number 11.

In 1991, I had the exceptional opportunity to drive Ken Miles' original special, R-1. Pat Hart, who owned this historic car, let me race it at Monterey and Sears Point. While I use the word race, I really took it very easy. After all, I was not experienced in such a high-powered vehicle, which was worth half a million dollars, and had no roll bar. It was a rare opportunity, and I thoroughly enjoyed the experience. As usual, I finished mid-pack.

Al at speed in R-1.

After completing restoration of my Morgan three-wheeler (Chapter 22), I competed with it in more than 30 races, at Monterey, Sears Point, San Diego and Buttonwillow.

A couple of my racing experiences at Laguna Seca bear repeating. One year, on the opening lap of practice, the TC engine "swallowed" a valve. (The head broke off a valve and destroyed a piston). I was offered another engine, and, after removing the TC motor, found the replacement engine was worthless. I loaded my dismantled engine in the trailer and replaced the hood and radiator on the MG.

The following day, prior to my race, I suited up, put my crash helmet on, got into my engineless-MG and had my crew push me out to the pre-grid. When all the cars departed for the racetrack, I sat there in my motionless MG and yelled, "Push! Push!" My crew, including Lynda, pushed a bit, gave up, and several other crewmembers, responding to my frantic pleas, took over pushing. I yelled, "Faster! Faster!" Just before entering the racetrack, I stopped at the tech center.

The tech inspector walked over and I shouted, "Raise the hood – see what's wrong – they told me this thing was ready to race!"

The expression on the poor guy's face when he raised the hood, and found there was no engine, was indescribable! He, of course, did not know whether I knew there was no engine in the car. Later, I was presented with the Sears "Die Hard" award for making the best effort of the weekend!

What started as a "let's do it like we usta" event, with many cars being driven to and from the track, evolved into a much more sophisticated and expensive sport, with the paddock crowded with huge car haulers, professional crews and equipment.

In 1993, strictly as a spoof, I entered both my TC and 3-wheel Morgan. I packed both cars with tools, a few spare parts, plus my tent and camping gear, and towed the Morgan with the TC from Santa Barbara to Monterey. I raced both cars for the weekend, and towed back home on Monday. The TC had no trouble towing the Morgan and, needless to say, I created quite a stir when I arrived at the track. Later, I received the *Automobile Magazine* award, "The Way It Was."

The picture on the following page was taken as I pulled into the paddock.

I have thoroughly enjoyed my thirty-two years "behind the wheel." I've lived through some unforgettable experiences, suffered very few mechanical problems, and, most importantly, have made many lasting friendships. The guys with the big, fast, expensive cars may be very serious, but those of us in the Pre-War Group really do have *fun*!

In 2007, I said something I had been saying for several years, but at age eighty, I really meant – "This will be my last year to compete." After an enjoyable and trouble-free weekend of racing the TC at Laguna Seca, I am having second thoughts about retiring – yet.

Will Edgar Photo. 2007

After the last race on Saturday, at the usual Pre-War Group pit party, I was totally surprised to find everyone wearing a T-shirt with my picture and the caption, "Al Moss Farewell Tour – First Annual!" I guess they all know me – perhaps too well – so I imagine no one will be too surprised to learn that I'm now planning on entering again this year – 2008. This will definitely be my last race – again!

(Thanks to Scott Dames and Graham Wallis for providing the T-shirts. If I'm accepted, I'll bring them this year, another of my last...)

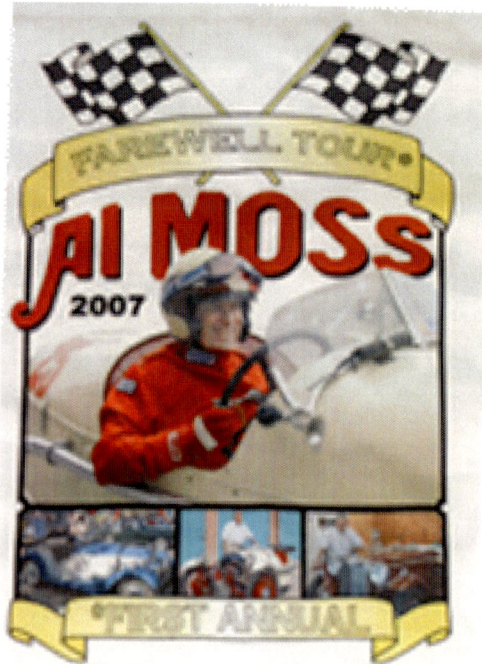

The T-shirt.

Following the last race on Sunday, there is an awards presentation. No awards are given for winning, but several special awards are given annually. In 2007, I was greatly pleased to be honored with the "Ken Miles Award." It is presented each year by Cy Yedor for "Outstanding Presentation of a Vintage Car under 1500cc." The award painting depicts Ken Miles driving his Flying Shingle, R-2, in the rain at Pebble Beach, followed by Cy Yedor in Ken's first MG Special, R-1.

THE KEN MILES AWARD
MONTEREY HISTORIC RACES
2007

FOR OUTSTANDING PRESENTATION
OF A VINTAGE CAR
UNDER 1500cc

PRESENTED BY CY YEDOR

I guess I can brag about the fact that while very few awards are presented annually at the Monterey Historic Races, I have been the fortunate recipient of several. In addition to the aforementioned Ken Miles Award, I received the Sears "Die Hard" Award (for showing up on the grid with my engineless MG), and the *Automobile Magazine* award, "The Way It Was" (for towing the Morgan with the TC and racing both). I also received the coveted Monterey Historic Award, "presented for outstanding restoration or presentation" (my Morgan).

*   *   *   *

As long as there is some extra space, how about a few old racing adages?

Winning isn't everything, but it sure as hell beats coming in second.

Dirt is for racing – Asphalt is for sissies.

To finish first – you must first finish.

There are no if's in motor racing.

and, my favorite –

You must be cheating, because I'm cheating, and you're beating me.

21 Old Number 11

I n 1985, I entered my MG TC in the first revival of the Palm Springs road race and, while there, met with John (Johnny) von Neumann. John was an old friend, who began his racing career with an MG TD in the first Palm Springs race in 1950. He later had a repair shop in the San Fernando Valley, and became the West Coast importer of Volkswagen cars. (Several mutual friends had turned the whole VW deal down, saying, "Those things will never sell!") Johnny continued racing, and also began distributing Porsches and importing Ferrari automobiles.

After winning the first Pebble Beach road race in 1950 with his MG, Johnny modified the car several more times and was a consistent winner in the under 1500cc class – until Roger Barlow came out with his light and fast Simca Special. John then sold the MG, now known as Number 11 (his racing number), to Tracy Bird and Bumpy Bell from Tucson, Arizona. They raced the car successfully before selling it to Johnny's stepdaughter, Josie. She raced the car for a while before selling in back to John.

John's second car was a Porsche 356 that he lightened by removing the top! He applied his racing number, eleven, to this and all subsequent cars he drove. When I restored the MG Special, the number eleven was reassigned to it, and the present owner of the Porsche was assigned number seventeen.

Following is a photograph of both ex-von Neumann cars at the Monterey Historic races, most likely taken in 1987.

John von Neumann's first and second racing cars.

Getting back to my encounter with John at Palm Springs in 1985, the following conversations took place over the three days:

Me: "Hi, John. How are you?"

John: "Fine, Al, and you?"

"By the way, John, where is Old Number 11?"

"At my home in Switzerland. Do you want to buy it?"

"The last thing I need is another car" – (later) "How much do you want for it?"

John quotes a price.

"That's too much. Will you take _____?"

"All right."

So, we shook hands and John later arranged shipment to Los Angeles from Switzerland. When the car arrived it was transported from the harbor to Vasek Polak's large racing shop. On the appointed day, I met Vasek and John, wrote a check, loaded the car onto my trailer and drove back to Santa Barbara.

After arrival from Switzerland. Note the California license plate: "JVN 1."

After completely dismantling the car, I set about restoring it – exactly as it was, or would have been in 1950 – with no plastic tie-wraps, pop-rivets or other modern components.

I was fortunate in several respects; I had known the car from the beginning, and John's ex-wife, Eleanor, was still alive and was a great help in giving me photographs, and even the original, handmade steering wheel (which had been made by the immortal Mal Ord). Although Bumpy Bell had died, Tracy Bird was living in Texas, and Josie (von Neumann) Bigelow was living in Ojai, California. All of these people were extremely helpful in my quest for information pertaining to the car's originality and history. Jay Chamberlain, who had done work on the car, was also helpful.

I performed the complete restoration in a very short time, doing all of the work myself: rebuilding the engine, gearbox, chassis, suspension and running gear, fabricating many parts, and painting the body, fenders, etc.

This was truly an enjoyable and satisfying project, and I felt privileged to work on a very historic race car.

My first outing with the newly-restored MG Special was at the Palm Springs race weekend in 1986. Johnny von Neumann and Vasek Polak came to see the car, and Tracy Bird flew from Texas to see his old car in action.

I cannot begin to describe my feelings the first time I raced the car in the Monterey Historics, for I was driving a very historic MG in a race with many of the same cars it had competed against some forty years previously. It was an unforgettable experience.

After having the enjoyment of acquiring and restoring the car, and racing it for several years, I decided to part with it, selling it to my good friend Don Martine. Don has a small MG museum at his bed & breakfast facility in Pacific Grove, and has been actively racing MGs for many years. I'm happy to report that he's done a marvelous job of maintaining and successfully racing the car.

In May of 2006, Don gave me the honor of asking me to drive old No. 11 in an all-MG race meet in Hallett, Oklahoma. Unfortunately, while warming the car up for the qualifying race, the engine disintegrated and caught fire. Not my fault, but, needless to say, I felt bad that it happened with me behind the wheel. At least we went out in a blaze of glory!   Thanks, Don!

von Neumann sits in Number 11 at the first (1950) Pebble Beach race. The car still has the upholstery, steel wheels, doors and rear fenders.

22 Morgans (Cars, Not Horses)

In 1909, an English gentleman by the name of H.F.S. (Harry) Morgan designed and built a quaint three-wheeled car, which he named – surprise! – Morgan. The car proved to be successful in competition, and he began receiving orders for similar cars.

The little three-wheelers continued in production, with constant improvements, until the early 1950s. Production of the 4/4 Morgan began shortly before WW II. (4/4 = 4 cylinders and 4 wheels). Morgan has never built its own engines – using proprietary motorcycle engines in the three-wheelers, and various four-and eight-cylinder engines in the later four-wheel cars. Approximately forty- thousand three-wheelers were manufactured, of which around two thousand exist worldwide – an excellent five-percent survival rate.

Much of the three-wheeler's popularity was due to its being sold, licensed and raced as a motorcycle. The tax rate was much lower than that of an automobile, and a full driver's license was not required. Also, it sold for about the same price as a motorcycle and, having a top, offered a modicum of protection against the weather, thus appealing to many wives and girlfriends in rainy England.

Morgans are still being built, in the same factory, in Malvern, England. They are hand-built (largely to order), are available in America, and are very fast and expensive. Contrary to popular belief, Morgans never had wooden frames – like every make of car manufactured until the late 1930s, they had bodies and doors framed in wood, then covered in steel or aluminum. All chassis frames were made of steel. (OK, there have been a few cars throughout history with actual wood frames – Marcos, for example).

I had always been fascinated by Morgan three-wheelers, and in 1987, I had the opportunity to purchase one – a 1934 Super Sports with a Matchless motorcycle engine. The car was located in Monterey, California. Once I saw and drove it, I knew I had to have it – so a deal was concluded and I trailered it back to Santa Barbara.

When I got the car home and took a friend for a ride, the fuel line fell off the carburetor and sprayed gasoline on the hot engine. With flames shooting many feet toward the sky, I was fortunate to find a garden hose and put out the fire before any damage occurred. The little car was quite original, but in rather deplorable condition. I drove it very carefully a few more times prior to completely dismantling it: body, frame, engine and all running gear.

While I found the restoration challenging, I thoroughly enjoyed the project. Those parts unobtainable from the British Morgan Club, I fabricated in my machine shop. To form the body structure, it was necessary to make all new wood parts, some curved. I used as many of the original parts as possible, but found it necessary to have a new lower apron fabricated. The frame, as such, was made up of many small tubes, which I had to replace. I painted the car cream, with bright-red wheels and trim; the interior was done in red leather.

The restoration was completed in time for me to enter the 1990 Monterey Historics. The entry form stated that a current photograph of the car was required, so I submitted the following photo, saying it was as current as possible. This was only four months prior to the event; still I did get accepted! I guess Steve Earle knew me well enough to have confidence that I would have the car together and race-ready for the upcoming Monterey Historics.

The car performed flawlessly and, while quite a challenge to drive, I enjoyed it immensely. During the first few laps, I couldn't help feeling proud – there I was, at speed in a car I built myself, and was performing beautifully.

The Morgan was a difficult, and challenging, car to drive. It was very light, with ample horsepower and had more than ample torque (pulling power). Its three-speed gearbox had no synchromesh, and there were no instruments to worry the driver. Once the race was underway, I ran entirely in top gear, never having to shift gears, not even up the steep hill at Laguna Seca. Quite exciting going down the Corkscrew!

The Morgan, being British, had right-hand drive. The steering was extremely "fast," with only one-half turn, lock-to-lock. There was no foot throttle; three levers on the steering wheel controlled the engine speed, spark advance/retard, and choke. I once had the engine quit in the middle of a high-speed turn, but quickly discovered the cause – my sleeve had become caught on the choke lever!

The engine did not have a water pump; the water circulated by a principle, part magic, part accident, and part physics, called "thermo-siphon." It worked! – the engine never overheated.

The Matchless motorcycle engine that powered the car sat way out in front. The overhead-valve operating gear was exposed, and this always fascinated people who watched the valves opening and closing when the engine was idling.

I subsequently competed with the Morgan in over thirty events and, after having the pleasure of restoring, showing and racing the car for nineteen years, sold it to a Morgan friend in 2006. (And, yes, I do miss it!)

The finished product.

When I was nearly finished restoring the three-wheeler (they are also referred to as "trikes," "tripods," etc.), I started looking for another Morgan to restore. I bought a well-used, 1948 4/4 (also known as a "flat-rad," due to the shape of the radiator). This was actually a pre-war design and, as I learned to my dismay, a pretty crude,

or, as they say, "agricultural," motorcar. It was built with mechanical, rather than hydraulic, brakes, which only help slow the car a bit. The seating and driving position was uncomfortable, to say the least. Anyone who thinks an MG TC is hard riding, should try an early Morgan!

I completely dismantled the car and, after totally rebuilding the engine, gearbox, brakes, steering, chassis and all running gear, began work on the body. Had I previously known the condition of the body, I would never have begun the restoration. Typically British, there was considerable rust, terrible previous bodywork, huge amounts of Bondo, and most of the wood was too rotted to even use as samples. So, I purchased large amounts of ash timber and set about making all new wood pieces.

Once this was done, I installed the body on the frame — and then began the chore of realigning everything. I finally completed the job, after many years of hard work, and painted the car an attractive, two-tone blue and off-white. With a new tan top, side curtains, tonneau cover, and leather interior, I had a pretty sharp, original Morgan.

I showed the car a few times, garnering some nice trophies, and subsequently sold it at the prestigious RM auction in Phoenix in January, 2006. I entered the car with no reserve price, which meant I had to accept the high bid, regardless what it may have been. I had hoped to at least come home with the amount I had invested. You can imagine my elation when it sold for enough over my invested amount to reimburse me about one dollar for each hour of my time!

The day I purchased the 4/4.

The finished product. A real beauty!

It's obvious why they were called "Flat Rads."

While I still have my shop at home (complete, with a lathe, milling machine, welders and many, many tools), I am sure this will have been my last, total car restoration. I had a knee replacement a few years ago, making it difficult to "get down and get under."

*   *   *   *

On the following page are some photos from my glorious Morgan racing days. If they seem a bit small, it's probably because you need new specs.

23   The MG TC Van

After accumulating and hoarding new and used MG parts for many years, I finally had enough pieces to build an entire TC, except for the body.

In 1931, the MG factory converted an M-Type roadster into a "High Speed Service Van." I thought this was pretty cute and designed a similar body for an MG TC.

The MG factory "High Speed Service Van." 1931.

First, I assembled a small, plastic-model MG TC kit and built a van body on it. It looked all right, so I proceeded to construct a van body out of cardboard sheets and affixed it to my TC, cutting, trimming and taping until it looked proper. In the meantime, I assembled an engine, gearbox and all the chassis parts, using as many new components as possible. Unobtainable parts, I made in my shop. With great difficulty, I made and assembled the internal wood structure to support the body panels that went from the rear of the doors forward to the hood.

As soon as the chassis and forward body were completed, I attached the cardboard "box" to my TC, made a trailer hitch, and towed the completed chassis 140 miles to Dick Troutman's shop in Costa Mesa.

Note the Shorrock supercharger and the two gas tanks I made.

The cardboard mock-up body on my MG TC.

Dick Troutman was one of the top race car builders, having constructed, with Tom Barnes, the famous Troutman-Barnes Special, as well as numerous Indy cars and Lance Reventlow's Scarabs. Dick did a marvelous job of creating the van body to my specifications. When it was

finished, I towed the van back home with the TC and proceeded to complete the project.

I spent many hours on details such as the octagonal rear window frames – milling each piece out of solid brass and silver-soldering them all together. The glass windows had MG logos sandblasted on them. Don Torgeson made the leather upholstery and removable top. I paneled the van interior in wood and painted the car in proper MG brown and cream colors.

When finished, I had a brand new MG TC, absolutely original from the doors forward. I drove the van to several MG meets, entered it in a few concours and even used it for a "pit car" at the Monterey Historic races. In 1983, I drove it from Santa Barbara to Baltimore, Maryland, for the East Coast MG Gathering. I had installed a new, period, Shorrock supercharger; this helped immeasurably with more power when crossing the high, Rocky Mountain passes.

Building the van was a difficult, but gratifying project and I derived considerable satisfaction from driving and displaying an interesting and unusual vehicle.

I eventually sold the van to Pat Hart, and it now reposes in his family's museum in Washington State, along with a 1956 LeMans Austin Healey and an MGB roadster, both of which I restored, as well as Ken Miles' former MG race cars, R-1, and R-2 (the famous Flying Shingle.)

Note the octagonal rear windows.

* * * *

This MG TD pickup was constructed in 1953, from two wrecked TDs, by Chuck Reynolds and George Beavis for Richter Motors. I acquired and restored it in 1964. It is now owned by Moss Motors.

24 My Abode

When Nancy and I married in 1971, we purchased a two-acre parcel of land in Hope Ranch Park. Not actually a ranch, this semi-private community is located in Santa Barbara, between Highway 101 and the Pacific Ocean. This is a very "horsey" community, with a network of over thirty miles of riding trails, and a private beach – the only beach in California that *legally* allows horses.

We built a nice home, plus a stable with four stalls and storage for hay and a trailer. Later, I constructed an addition for car and parts storage. I built a perimeter post and rail fence around the property, and then welded pipe corrals for the horses. The house had an oversize garage/workshop, where I restored several cars.

Nancy and I divorced in 1985, and I continued living in the Hope Ranch house until 1997. Then, having become disenchanted with Santa Barbara (primarily because of too many people), and having explored other areas, I decided Sedona, Arizona, would be a nearly ideal place to live. So, I began searching for a suitable home.

I now have what is, to me, an ideal home. Situated on 1.2 acres, this two-story home has everything I want – magnificent views and a very large garage/workshop. I think there is also a kitchen!

Sedona, with a population of around twelve thousand people, and an elevation of 4500 feet, is located about 100 miles north of Phoenix. It is surrounded by National Forest and spectacular red-rock formations. Summer days are not too hot and winters sometimes see light snowfall.

After living in Sedona for ten years, I am completely satisfied with my decision to leave Santa Barbara. I was afraid I would miss the ocean, but being surrounded by the beautiful red rocks is equally satisfying to me.

My Sedona abode.

One of several views I enjoy from my home.

When I purchased the house, the great-room contained a pool table. I had never played pool, but began to learn the game. Pretty soon a group was formed of six Sedona Car Club friends, and we began shooting pool every Monday and Friday afternoon. Two other members have tables, so we are able to rotate amongst the three homes. We don't take the game too seriously, having four hours of camaraderie each session, interspersed with a mid-afternoon beer break.

"The Gang That Couldn't Shoot Straight."

I constructed a showcase for part of my model car collection. The leaded stained glass windows are from the old Morris Garages building in Oxford, England. Notice that the usual octagon does not surround the letters "MG". That came later.

For those uninitiated, I offer this – MG stands for Morris Garages, not Mother Goose or My God! The first MGs were built at Morris Garages, hence the name.

The Moss Museum of historic race cars.

Some of the many awards I have won with cars and horses.

Somewhere in the Rocky Mountains.

25 Interesting People

During my long and "illustrious" career, I have had the pleasure of meeting quite a few well-known personalities in the automotive field. Some I met only briefly, others I got to know fairly well. In no particular order, a few of these people are described here.

Ab Jenkins was the former mayor of Salt Lake City and holder of many long distance records on the Salt Flats of Bonneville, Utah, driving his famous Mormon Meteors, which he designed and had built on Duesenberg chassis. I met and spent some time talking with Ab in 1950, at the first Motorama show in Los Angeles. He explained to me that he not only held records in automobiles, but on tractors as well! Over the long period of his racing career, he held and broke more long-distance speed records than any other person in the history of motor sports.

Cecil Cousins and Alec Hounslow. Both longtime employees of the MG factory, Cecil was the first employee at MG, and later became plant manager. Alec was a racing mechanic and was riding mechanic with the great Tazio Nuvolari when they won their class in the 1933, Ulster, Tourist Trophy race, driving a supercharged MG K3 Magnette. Alec spoke no Italian and Tazio no English, but somehow Alec had to teach Tazio how to handle the tricky Wilson pre-selector gearbox in the Magnette!

Captain George Eyston. This fine British gentleman raced many different cars and set a great many world speed records. Accompanied by Count Johnny Lurani, in 1933 he won his class in the grueling Mille Miglia, a 1000-mile race around Italy, driving a K-3 MG Magnette. I enjoyed the time I spent chatting with him, both in England and on the East Coast. Eyston broke the Land Speed Record several times, achieving 357.50 miles per hour in "Thunderbolt" at Bonneville, in 1938.

Chatting with Captain George Eyston at the MG factory.

John Thornley OBE (Order of the British Empire). John became secretary of the newly-formed MG Car Club in 1930. and joined the MG Car Company the following year. By 1955, he had worked his way up to managing director, a position he held until 1968, his retirement year.

I first met John in his office, the day before his retirement from MG. We had a nice, long chat and I took the following photograph with no flash, on a dark and rainy day.

Later, after his retirement, John, his wife, Ann, and I became close friends. During many of my trips to England, I was a guest in their lovely Abingdon home – where we enjoyed good times, meals and drinks together. John was perhaps the most intelligent person I have ever known; he also possessed a great sense of humour.

Allow me to share a few memories.

John was provided with free petrol by the MG factory, so one afternoon we drove there to fill up. While John was filling the car, I ran upstairs to the drawing office. As it was near closing time, someone asked if they could drive me home. I replied. "No thanks; my driver will be up shortly." They were a bit surprised a few moments later when John Thornley walked in and asked if I was about ready to leave!

In 1979, the GoF-West steering committee flew John and Ann to California, to be guests of honor at the MG gathering in San Diego. Nancy and I picked them up in San Francisco. Mrs. Kjell (Kay) Qvale gave us a tour of San Francisco in her beautiful Rolls Royce. That evening we enjoyed a sumptuous dinner at the Qvale house. We then spent two days in the redwoods, drove south to visit Hearst Castle, and then spent a few enjoyable days at our home in Santa Barbara, before journeying to San Diego – all four of us in my 1949 MG sedan.

In addition to having the Thornleys as our guests at the MG meet, we also invited Phil and Alma Hill as special guests. We managed to have EX181 on display. This was the MG-powered, streamlined car, named "The Roaring Raindrop," which, in 1959, Phil drove to a world record speed of 254.91 mph on the Bonneville Salt Flats. Phil climbed into the EX181 and described his experiences while driving the car at high speed on the salt flats.

Phil explains some of the finer points of EX181 to John and me.

EX181. The 'Roaring Raindrop'. (254.91 mph)

In 1950, John wrote what is definitely the best of many books published about the MG marque. Titled *"Maintaining The Breed,"* (the factory slogan). this book has been reprinted several times. During his stay in my home in 1979, John paid me the highest compliment I ever received, when he penned the following inscription in my copy of his book.

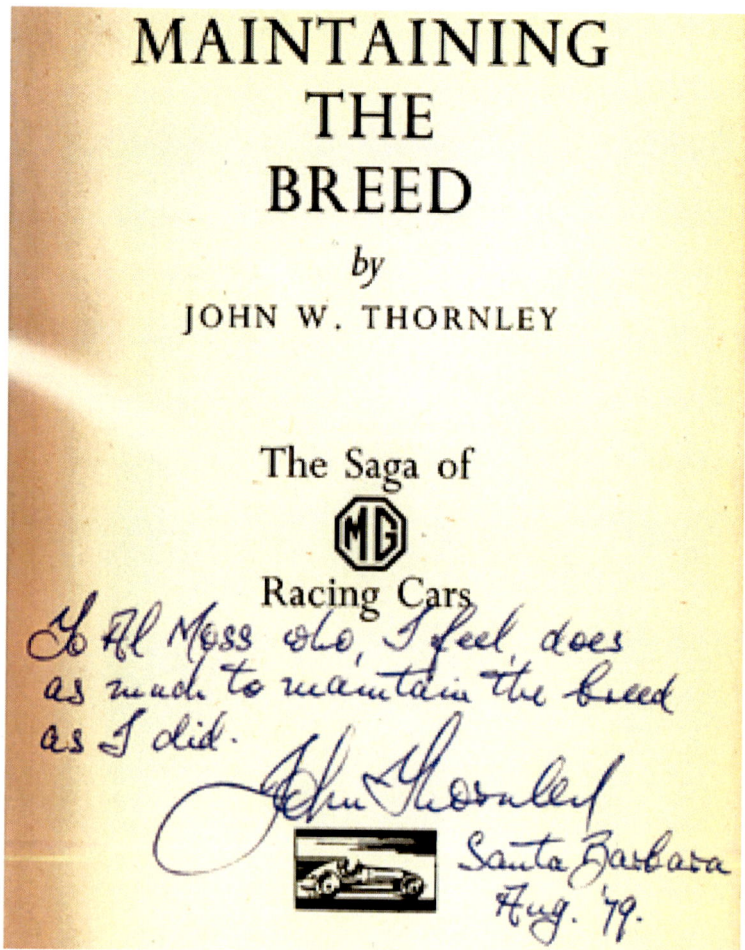

MAINTAINING
THE
BREED

by

JOHN W. THORNLEY

The Saga of

MG

Racing Cars

To Al Moss who, I feel, does as much to maintain the breed as I did.

John Thornley

Santa Barbara
Aug. '79.

John and Ann sold their lovely home in Abingdon-on-Thames around 1984 and moved south to Somerset. All English houses have names and theirs was called *The Barn*, for obvious reasons — it *had* been a barn many years ago, and is a beautiful country home today.

Here is a picture of Ann and John with Bimbo, which I took in 1987 when Lynda and I stayed with the Thornleys.

John, Ann and Bimbo in their garden at "The Barn."

This was the last time I saw John. Sadly, he passed away in 1994 at the age of 85. Ann later remarried and is now living in the United States.

Donald Healey. Born in 1898, Healey survived being shot down in WW1. He went on to great success in Monte Carlo rallies, winning in 1931, while driving an Invicta. He developed the line of Healey cars, from the Sprite to the 3000 as well as the Nash Healey. Donald visited Santa Barbara shortly before his death in 1988, and I had the pleasure of meeting him and showing him my recently re-

stored LeMans Healey Hundred. I discussed with him the possibility of us getting together with John Thornley on my next visit to England, but this never came to fruition. Donald was a most charming and interesting individual.

Donald Healey in my 1956 LeMans Healey Hundred.

Peter Morgan. Peter's father, H.F.S. Morgan, was the founder of the Morgan Car Company. Peter ran the company from 1959 until the time of his death. I was racing my Morgan at Monterey in 2003, and had the opportunity of meeting and chatting with this fine gentleman in my pit. He proved to have a good sense of humor and laughed when I showed him my non-original fender brace that had broken – I asked him if it was still under warranty.

When I mentioned my car's severe vibration, he drew to full height and said, "Remember, Mr. Moss – we at Morgan *never* built an engine!"

A pity, Peter Morgan passed away two months later, at the age of 84.

With Peter Morgan at Monterey, August, 2003.

Henry Stone. Henry was a racing mechanic with the MG Car Company most of his life. We became close friends and had some great times together, both in California and in the U.K. Henry, and his gracious wife, Winnie, came to California twice, as guests at our MG gatherings. On one of these trips they stayed at our Hope Ranch house for several days, and enjoyed relaxing on the beach. I was a guest, several times, in their Abingdon home, which was close to the MG factory. Henry and I downed many a pint together at the nearby Magic Midget pub.

Ralph De Palma. A great driver in early races, both here and abroad, he was winner of the Indianapolis 500 in 1915, and approximately 2000 other races in his 25-year career. Mr. De Palma was honorary starter for some of our early Cal Club races in Southern California, and I had occasion to speak with him frequently during those times.

Peter De Paolo. Ralph DePalma's nephew, Pete, started his automobile racing career as a riding mechanic for Uncle Ralph, and went on to be a top driver in his own right. Driving a Duesenberg, he won the 1925, Indianapolis 500 race, the first time the winning speed exceeded 100 miles an hour. After World War II, he managed the Ford team effort in stock car racing. When Kjell Qvale got into big-time racing with the MG Liquid Suspension Specials, Pete was in charge of that operation. The last time I saw him was at Qvale's office in San Francisco.

Pat O'Connor. I had the pleasure of meeting and sitting next to this popular and prominent Indy car driver at dinner one evening, shortly before he was killed (due to an accident, not his fault) at the start of the 1958 Indy 500.

Jim Hurtibise. I got to know Jim when we both hung out at my neighbor's garage. I spent many evenings watching Gus Linhares work on his two Offy midgets, one of which Jim occasionally drove. It was here that Jim acquired his nickname, "Hercules." I once let Jim ride my 650 Triumph motorcycle, something I don't usually allow.

Al Unser, Sr. When I raced my TC at the Monterey Historics in 2007, I was pitted across from a large Lagonda that was being driven by four-time Indy winner, Al Unser. I went over to meet him and explained that, as this was his first time racing in the Monterey Historics, he needed to know some rules he must follow. Pointing to my MG, I told him he was not to pass that car. He laughed, and in the race, gave me a cheery wave each time he passed me. We chatted again after our race, and I told him that he owed me some money. "What for?" he asked.

"Because I paid for ten laps and you passed me twice, so I only got eight laps!" He laughed! I was impressed by what a really nice guy he is.

During the formative years of California road racing, I spent a lot of time getting to know nearly all of the drivers, some very well and some only as nodding acquaintances. Quite a few of these men went on to achieve fame in various forms of motor sport, including the pinnacle of racing – Formula One (or Grand Prix).

Ken Miles. Undoubtedly the finest driver on the West Coast, he never raced in Formula One, but achieved considerable success in all forms of sports car racing. He nearly won the Le Mans 24-hour race in 1964, and should have. Ken met an untimely death at age 48, testing a Ford "J-Car" at Riverside, in 1966.

For several years, I enjoyed a friendship with Ken and his supportive wife, Molly, and for nine months, it was my privilege to crew for him when he was racing his first MG special, R-1. I had nothing to do with the car, but did Ken's timing, signaling and strategy. All I can say is that I learned he was one helluva fine driver! I remain in contact with Ken and Molly's son, Peter, who I knew as a young lad when Ken was racing.

Jack McAfee. Known by his friends as Jack the Bear, Jack was, in spite of being a fierce competitor, one of the kindest drivers I have had the pleasure of knowing. I'll give an example of this.

I was taking photos at a remote turn during a Bakersfield airport race when, directly opposite me, a driver rolled his Austin Healey and was trapped underneath. There was no telephone nearby, and no one else was around, when Jack, who was leading the race in his Ferrari, approached. I motioned him to a stop and asked him to summon help at the start/finish line, which he did. How many drivers, then, and especially now, would jeopardize their lead to help someone else?

Jack began his career with hot rods and became involved with sports cars in the late forties. He drove in most of the 1950's Mexican Road Races, and went on to become one of the top Porsche and Ferarri drivers. Sadly, Jack passed away in March of 2007.

Ernie McAfee. No relation to Jack, they were good friends and both were competent mechanics as well as topnotch drivers. The finest bit of racing I have ever seen was one practice day at Santa Barbara with Ernie, Jack and Phil Hill in big, fast Ferraris. I lost track of how many times they passed and repassed each other, but I could tell they were having a great time of it. Unfortunately, in 1956, Ernie was killed when his Ferrari hit a tree at what became, the final Pebble Beach Road Race.

Pete Lovely. Pete has been actively racing since the early fifties and still enjoys his racing activities. He started in sports cars, most famously his "Pooper," a former Grand Prix Cooper with a Porsche engine in the rear. Pete graduated to, and competed in, eleven Formula One races in the 1950's, -- and won the inaugural Laguna Seca race in 1951. He was a VW dealer in Tacoma, Washington, and now operates a restoration shop, specializing in historic racing cars, and he currently races his Lotus 49B.

Max & Ina Balchowsky. Two of the real stalwarts of early California road racing, Max and Ina were the creators of, among many other cars, the series of "Old Yellers", which graced the racing circuit for many years.

The couple operated a shop in Hollywood and worked together repairing, designing and building race cars. Ina was a top mechanic in her own right and, so goes the story, she had Max sit on the shop floor while she drew chalk lines around him, thereby designing a new chassis for the next special – which was built with whatever parts were handy, using Chevrolet or Buick engines.

Named "Old Yeller," after the Disney movie about a dog, these cars (always fitted with white sidewall tires) won many races, often beating expensive Ferraris and Maseratis. Several future driving stars, like Dan Gurney, Phil Hill, Dave MacDonald and the two Bobs, Drake and Bondurant, often drove Old Yellers to victory.

Backing up a bit, in 1952, when I was Chief Technical Inspector, I received a telephone call from Cal Club headquarters. informing me that they had received an entry application they wanted me to turn down. I asked for an explanation and was informed that the applicant wanted to enter a – *hot rod*! Sports car owners tended think of hot-rods as being inferior to expensive, imported sports cars. This seemed quite snobbish to me. So, my response was, "Please clarify the difference between a hot rod and an Allard." (After all, the Allard started out as a British "hot rod").

The application had included a photograph of a 1932 Ford roadster, with a dog sitting in front of the car. I phoned the applicant, Max Balchowsky, and suggested he bring the car to my shop for a pre-race examination. I found several things that did not comply with our regulations: no emergency brake, improper fender width, etc. Max corrected these irregularities, entered the next race, and a short time later, became one of our most popular and respected competitors.

Following success with his Buick-powered, 1932 Ford roadster, Max stuffed a Buick engine in a new Doretti and raced this for a few years before building what became Old Yeller Mk I. I grew to know Ina and Max quite well, and was very sad when they both passed away a few years ago.

The following photo of Max and Ina is one of my favorites. It shows them both tuning Old Yeller at a Riverside race in October 1961.

Phil Hill. Phil and I started out in MG TCs in 1948. Phil had a natural talent for driving race cars and achieved success in all forms of motor racing. Ultimately, while driving for Ferrari, Phil became the second American to win a Grand Prix and, in 1961, the first American to win the World Driver's Championship. Phil was also a noted endurance driver, winning the Le Mans twenty-four-hour race and the twelve-hours of Sebring – three times each. Outstanding achievements for a fellow Californian – a man I am proud to have as a friend.

I felt pleased and honored to receive an invitation to Phil's 80th birthday party. He turned eighty on April 20, 2007, and the party was held that night at Jay Leno's Big Dog Garage in Burbank. This was one fantastic evening!

Jay allowed us to roam freely through his private car collection, occupying a total of 17,000 square feet in several adjacent buildings. I was like a kid in a candy store, especially when Jay said it was OK to freely photograph his cars and motorcycles. A real privilege, as this is a private collection, and is not normally open to the public

In addition to Phil and his charming family, and quite a few of Phil's contemporary drivers and their families, prominent people from all over the world were in attendance. Some of Phil's friends who were unable to attend sent brief video messages that were displayed on huge screens in the theater. This was, by far, one of the most enjoyable evenings I have ever spent. Thanks, Phil and Alma, for inviting me.

Roger Barlow co-owned International Motors, with several branches in Hollywood. In 1951 he designed a special, using a Simca 1200cc engine with a beautiful body built by Emil Deidt. Being very light (around 1000 pounds) and well driven by Roger, this and a second similar car swept everything in the under-1500 cc races on the West Coast for several years.

After the demise of International Motors, I became close friends with Roger and his wife, Louise. They moved back to Virginia where Louise passed away in the 1960s. Roger later remarried and I visited him and Mary several times in their New Market home. In addition to his many automotive exploits, Roger was a talented photographer and writer. Roger passed away in 1990.

And let's not forget Richie Ginther. Richie was one of "the gang" in our early California racing days. He was talented driver, and an expert mechanic. A close friend of Phil Hill, Richie co-drove with Phil in two of the early Mexican road races, and later graduated to Formula One. He drove for Ferrari and then for Honda, giving both him

and Honda their first Grand Prix win. My last and lasting recollection of Richie was when, during one our post-race parties in Santa Barbara, my daughter put Richie on her Shetland pony and turned the pair loose in the house. They wandered all through the house, with Richie saying, "How do you steer this damn thing?" And no one had a camera!

Various other interesting people. At another one of our post-race parties my kids let Dick Smother's wife, Linda, loose in the house on my Arabian horse! Lots of fun in those long-gone days.

Following are a few other well-known drivers I met, albeit briefly: Sir Stirling Moss, Juan Manuel Fangio (5 times World Champion), Froilan Gonzalez, Sir Jack Brabham, Carroll Shelby, Bob Bondurant and Dan Gurney.

I also became acquainted with several older, prominent, British race drivers, including Rivers Fletcher, Denis Evans, Dudley Froy and Faye Taylour.

Queen Elizabeth. The British monarch is by far the most famous person I have ever met. During her visit to Santa Barbara, on March 1st, 1983, she made a formal appearance at the Santa Barbara Courthouse. I was dressed in costume to represent Gaspar de Portola, the Spanish explorer who led an expedition from San Diego, through Monterey, to San Francisco – where he discovered San Francisco Bay. That was in 1768, the same year he was appointed Governor of California. The Queen, accompanied by the Mayor, stopped and asked me whom I was representing. Luckily, I knew, and gave her a brief explanation. She thanked me and went on her way.

I was bitterly disappointed when the Queen didn't ask for my autograph.

26   The Astronauts

In the early part of 1973, Colonel Gerald Carr, who arrived at the nearby Santa Barbara Airport by military jet, paid me a visit at Moss Motors. "Jerry" was involved in the development and testing of the Lunar Rover, which was being built at adjacent General Motors-Delco, where they had a replica lunar landscape.

Another (the main?) reason for the astronaut's visit was to meet me and discuss his 1952 MG TD. We had a most enjoyable visit and I provided him with some parts he needed.

I was under the impression that Colonel Carr was going to drive the Lunar Rover on its first space visit. But, plans apparently changed and he became commander of the three-man crew on an 84-day visit to Skylab 4, the longest space visit at that time. Accompanying him on the mission were Dr. Edward Gibson (science pilot) and William R. Pogue (pilot).

I was pleasantly surprised to receive three photographs from Colonel Carr. The first was taken by *National Geographic* for an article about the mission. Unfortunately, this photograph did not appear in the article.

These photos and inscriptions are very special to me, and I am proud to share them with you, dear reader.

The inscription on the top photo reads, "To Al Moss. Our warmest wishes." (signed) Jerry Carr, Ed Gibson and Bill Pogue. The inscription on the second reads, "The classic MG is alive and well in Texas," – "My best wishes, Jerry Carr. Skylab III."

To Al Moss —
The classic MG is alive and well in Texas!

My best wishes,
Jerry Carr

"To my good friends at Moss Motors. Many thanks for helping me keep my TD on the road. Jerry Carr."

As an aside, when the Moss Motors office staff (all women) got wind that A REAL LIVE ASTRONAUT was coming to visit, the ladies got spruced up and one woman ran home and brought her kids back. Prior to Carr's arrival, I couldn't resist dressing our cleanup boy in a crash helmet, gloves and a raincoat on backwards. I then announced on the intercom that the astronaut was coming in. The staff sat up straight, looking attentive. When the door opened and the aberration was led in, their surprised looks were apparent, but they had become accustomed to my shenanigans.

Later, during his actual visit, Carr laughed when I told him about this.

27 Motor Museums

I have had the privilege of visiting many automobile museums and will describe some of them, in no particular order.

Harrah's Collection. William "Bill" Harrah amassed a collection of approximately 1500 cars in a huge warehouse in Sparks, Nevada, just outside of Reno. In 1975, Nancy and I were driving the TC to Bend, Oregon, for the MG gathering, and on the way were treated to a personal tour of the facility by my good friend, the late Dean Batchelor.

Bill Harrah, who died in 1978, was a true car enthusiast and it was surprising that he left no provision in his will to perpetuate the collection. The entire Harrah Empire was acquired by the Holiday (Inn) Corporation. They sold most of the cars, the remaining 200 becoming the basis for the National Automobile Museum in Reno. Lynda and I visited this impressive museum in 1999, during an MGA meet.

The Schlumpf Collection. The Schlumpf Brothers, Hans and Fritz, were wealthy owners of several textile mills in Mulhouse, in the Alsace region of France. The brothers were avid automobile collectors and amassed a huge assortment of exotic European racing and classic cars. Being particularly enamored with the marque Bugatti, they managed to acquire 123 Bugattis, including two of the six Royales.

They had their 200,000 square foot museum nearly completed, when the textile business failed, the employees took over the museum and the brothers Schlumph fled the country.

Ultimately, a consortium took over the museum, and it is now open to the public. The cars are magnificently displayed, and the building houses a restaurant and gift shop.

There are 400 cars on display, plus another 140 in reserve.

In 1978, during the time the employees occupied the museum, I drove through Belgium, Germany and France in hopes of getting into the museum. Fortunately, after listening to unintelligible speeches in French by two of the disgruntled ex-employees who had taken over the museum, a few of us were allowed inside, and I spent several hours ogling and photographing the cars. This is one of the largest automobile museums in the world and it was well worth the effort to get there.

Bugattis — Bugattis — as far as the eye can see.

Mercedes-Benz Museum. Located in Stuttgart, Germany, this museum houses over 100 Mercedes-Benz cars, including many classic models, as well as historic racing and record-setting cars.

I wanted to visit this museum on the way to Mulhouse, but found that it was temporarily closed to the public. While in England, I made a few phone calls and received credentials to enter it and take as many photos as I desired. It was a most enjoyable experience. Recently, in Stuttgart, Mercedes constructed a beautiful, ultramodern, multi-story building containing 160 vehicles.

Porsche Museum. As it is located not far from the Mercedes-Benz Museum in Stuttgart, I paid a brief visit to this small, compact collection, displaying approximately twenty cars. (After all, Porsche, having started in 1939, is a relatively new company.) On display were some late model racing cars, a few early 356 models, and a few Austro-Daimlers, which were designed by Dr. Ferdinand Porsche.

National Motor Museum (Beaulieu). Located in England's New Forest, this museum evolved from the Montagu Motor Museum, founded in 1952, by Lord Edward Montagu as a tribute to his father, John Scott Montagu, one of Britain's motoring pioneers. On permanent display are over 250 cars and motorcycles, many of great historic value. The grounds are the location of the annual Beaulieu Autojumble, equal in size and scope to our Hershey and Carlisle swap meets. It was here that I had the honor of meeting and talking to the charming Lord Montagu.

Scottish Museums. I spent a lovely weekend in and around the North Sea town of Dunbar, the birthplace of John Muir. My reason for going there was to visit a small, semi-private car collection. The rare and unusual cars were the property of the late Willie Dale.

After leaving Dunbar, I made the short drive along the coast to the tiny town of Aberlady, where the balance of the collection was housed in two buildings on the late owner's farm. One nice thing about these two small museums is that visitors are allowed to *touch* the cars, even sit in them and raise the hoods. All the cars are well maintained and driven regularly.

California Museums. I have also had the pleasure of visiting the prime automotive museums in California, many times. These include:

The Blackhawk Museum. Located in Blackhawk, near Danville, not far from San Francisco, this collection was established by Ken Behring, and later turned over to the University of California. The three times I visited, the museum contained about 70 cars, each displayed in a totally black environment, with low-key lighting. All of the cars, many of them Pebble Beach Concours winners, are in magnificent condition and are frequently driven.

Chandler Museum. Located in Oxnard, between Santa Barbara and Los Angeles, this now-defunct museum was established by the late Otis Chandler, owner and publisher of the *Los Angeles Times* newspaper. Chandler was an avid car enthusiast, whose interests ranged from motorcycles to exotic cars, as well as to big game hunting. He drove in many races and won an event at Riverside a few years ago. His museum, containing about 50 cars and 40 motorcycles, was never open to the general public – only to car clubs by invitation. I arranged a few tours, and each time met and chatted with Mr. Chandler (please call me "Otis"). He made it a point to apologize for his vast displays of wild-animal trophies, saying he shot them long before the current outcry against this "sport." He later did his "hunting" with cameras. Otis passed away in 2006 and the collection went to auction. At last report, the buildings have been purchased by collector and vintage racer Peter Mullen, to be used for???

Petersen Museum. Located in the heart of Los Angeles, at Wilshire and Fairfax, this multi-story museum was established in 1994, by Robert "Pete" Petersen, founder and publisher of *Hot Rod, Motor Trend and Auto*, as well as many other magazines. The four-story building houses about half of the museum's 200 cars. I knew Pete quite well in the early days of *Hot Rod* magazine and was one of his staff photographers. Pete passed away in 2007, but the museum continues to remain open to the public.

Nethercutt (San Sylmar) Museum. Established in 1956 by avid car enthusiasts, Jack and Dorothy Nethercutt, this beautiful facility, located in Sylmar, California (a few miles north of Los Angeles), consists of two large buildings. The original building has three levels, the main floor being a replica of an art deco, 1930s auto showroom. The top floor contains a large collection of operable, antique, mechanical musical instruments, as well as car mascots, badges and Lalique crystal. Occasionally on display is a far-from-original, but beautiful, MG TC which Mike Goodman and I restored in 1963.

The Nethercutts owned Merle Norman Cosmetics. They named their museum San Sylmar, a takeoff on William Randolph Hearst's, "San Simeon."

Two of our finest automotive museums reside in Indiana. Many years ago, Auburn, Indiana, was known as the automobile capital of the world. A great number of now-extinct makes were manufactured there. Among the finest of these were Auburn, Cord and Duesenberg – all three ultimately being under the ownership of E. L. Cord.

The Auburn-Cord-Duesenberg Museum is located in the town of Auburn in a two-story, art deco building. Originally built in 1930 as an Auburn showroom, it once had offices on the second floor, but those are now devoted to automotive memorabilia, and mannequins, dressed in period clothing. This magnificent building is home to approximately 100 beautifully restored examples of the three marques, some the property of private owners.

The Indianapolis Motor Speedway Hall of Fame Museum is located in the infield of the famous speedway. Beautifully displayed inside are 75 historic, mostly American, race cars and memorabilia. The winner of the first Indy 500 race in 1911, the Marmon 'Wasp', driven by Ray Harroun, is on display, as is the famous Borg-Warner trophy.

On a cold, rainy day in 1981, I was driving west on the interstate highway between Spokane and Portland, when I noticed a large barn on the opposite side of the interstate. On top of the building, in large letters, were two magic words: *OLD CARS.*

I was not terribly surprised when my car, with no input from me, exited at the next off ramp, crossed over the interstate and went straight back to the barn.

No one was around, so I pressed a button, a horn honked, and out from the house came a very old man. He approached and said, "I suppose you want to see my cars."

"Yes, please, what do you have."? The answer came as a surprise.

"Hudsons!"

He opened the door, and there, to my amazement, stood over 125 Hudson cars and Hudson derivatives (Terraplane, Essex, Rambler, etc.) The old gentleman explained that he follows ads from all over the country and buys these cars cheaply because, "no one else wants them." He claimed that all of his cars ran. I often wonder what happened to this collection. I'm sure the old gent is not still around to enjoy his toys.

Great Britain. In addition to the previously mentioned museums, I visited a number of other car and motorcycle museums in Great Britain, including the Isle of Man. The following were outstanding:

The National Motorcycle Museum. Opened in 1984, this museum, located in Birmingham, consisted of four or five halls, each containing displays of a particular era, marque or form of motorcycling. I made several visits to this facility, and was always amazed at the scope and quality of the many rare bikes on display. Unfortunately, in

September, 2003 a cigarette-caused fire destroyed about 60% of the facility and motorcycles.

Donington Collection. Located near Derby, in the Midlands, this collection of over 130 historic race cars and related exhibits is housed in five buildings. Several years ago, Tom Wheatcroft, a wealthy contractor, acquired Donington Park, situated on the grounds of Donington Castle. He not only built the buildings to house the collection, he also restored the prewar, Donington Park racing circuit, where Grand Prix races were held before the war, and racing has once again resumed.

Of all the automotive museums I have visited, Donington is, by far, my favorite.

Unique Museum Cars. Of the many different makes and models of automobiles produced over the years, the largest, heaviest, most expensive and most powerful, were the six Bugatti Royales (Type 41), built in 1931 and priced at $42,000 to $45,000. (Present value – eight to ten million dollars).

I was privileged to see all six of these cars in the 1970s: two at the Schlumph Museum in France, one at the Henry Ford Museum in Dearborn, one at the former Briggs Cunningham Museum in Costa Mesa, and two at the former Harrah's Automobile Collection in Reno.

*   *   *   *

Looking back, I realize how fortunate I've been to have traveled to all these wonderful automobile museums and witnessed, first hand, so many unforgettable vehicles.

Information on these museums is available on the web – just Google the name of the museum.

*   *   *   *

The Indianapolis 500

While not really a museum experience, in 1990, I was able to fulfill a long-standing dream. Since childhood, I have followed the Indianapolis 500 race, first on radio and later on television, but I always yearned to be there in person for at least one race, so I decided to drive to the event. Thanks to help from a fellow MG TC owner who lives near the Speedway, I had a good seat and a nice place to stay within walking distance of the Speedway.

Leaving Santa Barbara early on the Sunday preceding the race, I drove straight through in my new Nissan 300ZX, camping out each night. I arrived Wednesday noon and, after meeting my friend, we ate lunch at the Speedway Motel Restaurant, amid many of the drivers and crews.

In spite of excellent weather and an excellent seat, my overall impression was that it probably was not worth spending two weeks, fifteen hundred dollars and making a drive of nearly five thousand miles to see only one part of the huge track. The only way I could follow the action was by listening to the radio broadcast on my Sony Walkman! The Indy 500 became less interesting to me after the demise of the Offenhauser Roadsters, so I'm not sure why I even went! It was nice to soak up the atmosphere, but I prefer watching the race live on TV.

I did thoroughly enjoy watching the midget car races at Indianapolis Raceway Park, the night before the 500. A very young Jeff Gordon won every event that night — I could see a star in the making.

28 Humor

Apparently I was born with a sense of humor, which I probably inherited from my mother. For example, I remember the time my father planted a small banana tree in the yard and Mom went out late at night and tied a few bananas to the branches.

Therefore, I enjoy a good, harmless practical joke, whether reading about one, playing one, or having one played on me. My idea of a successful practical joke is one that creates a good laugh without hurting anyone's feelings or property.

For starters, in 1976, at the conclusion of the Bicentennial Rally in Philadelphia, I had occasion to go to my third-floor room during the awards banquet. On the way down the hall, I noticed that all of the room numbers were attached to the doors with small screws. As I happened to have a tool kit in the room, I grabbed a screwdriver and quickly changed the room numbers from door to door. Later, I heard comments as people were returning to their rooms. Like, "I am sure the door handle was on the other side before we went to dinner." Lots of laughs were had by all and, naturally, I got the blame.

Then there was the GoF in San Diego, where I sneaked into the banquet room prior to dinner and went to each table with super glue. I placed a drop between a cup and saucer, between a wine glass and plate, between a salt- and pepper-shaker, under a fork resting on a knife. Sitting at the head table, I could see my efforts unfolding all through the banquet. Got blamed for that, too, of course!

Even the police were fair game! A very nice, local policeman, Gene, used to drop by my Los Angeles shop frequently. One Saturday morning, while he was talking with a few customers, I crept under the back of his police car and jacked one wheel slightly off the ground. When he

attempted to leave, he was dismayed to find the car would not move, until I released the jack.

Another day, I received a call in my office from a man sounding like a Mafia member. He said he would be in town tomorrow and would come to see me about unionizing Moss Motors. Needless to say, I panicked and called an attorney for advice. It was a while before I learned a friend of a friend made the call.

One of the best and longest-lasting gags, however, involved Henrietta Glockenspiel.

In 1957, I was driving the TC in Hollywood and spied a mannequin for sale. After paying six dollars, I dismantled "her" and drove her to my house in the back of the TC. The look on my very young daughter, Cindy's, face as I reassembled Henrietta was priceless. She had no idea this was how women were created!

Henrietta spent time at Moss Motors and later did quite a bit of traveling. One time a few folks in an East Coast MG club arranged a blind date between Henrietta and a bachelor member for the club's annual banquet. After buying Henrietta a nice traveling outfit (at Salvation Army), she was duly crated and shipped off for her big evening. I was sorry not to have been there to see her presented. Seems her escort-to-be was flitting from table to table telling everyone about his blind date, when the door opened and Henrietta was wheeled in. Poor Earl. He had even polished his Porsche for the big occasion.

The following two pictures show Henrietta all dressed in her finery, ready to travel east for her big date. How she became pregnant is a mystery. At an East Coast GoF, someone posed Henrietta at Abingdon Spares booth. Abingdon was a competitor of Moss Motors, and I posed with the sign as a gag. Later, Henrietta was hung from the ceiling in the chairman's room by a cord – the Hispanic maid went down the hall screaming, "Lady hang!"

In 1993, I designed and manufactured an oil seal kit for the rear of MG engines. I was pretty excited about this project and installed the first one in my TC. Lynda and I were on our way from Santa Barbara to Arizona with some MG friends, and every time we stopped I took a quick peek under the TC and was dismayed to see a puddle of oil on the ground. It appeared to be leaking worse than before I installed the new seal. A few days later the truth emerged. Lynda had kept me distracted while a nameless friend poured oil under the car at each stop!

Incidentally, after a few "teething" problems were solved, these kits proved to be successful and over 2900 have been sold to date. No more MG oil puddles!

In 1982, some "friends" completely wrapped my motorcycle in toilet paper, tied balloons all over it, and then hoisted it way up an oak tree. The sign said, "You meet the nicest people on a Honda." After I cut it down, I was quite a sight – riding around with balloons and T.P. flapping in the breeze.

The MGs, like most "Briddish" cars, had an electric fuel pump mounted under the hood. A favorite joke was to undo the wire from the pump. The owner would get in his car, start it up and drive about two blocks, only to have the engine stop when the fuel in the carburetors was used up – the car, seemingly, out of gas.

A memorable event occurred at a GoF in San Diego. A well-organized crew came prepared, with a duplicate key to my MG sedan, as well as sacks of those horrible Styrofoam pellets. They opened the sunroof, and filled the interior clear to the top with the pellets. A great gag with no harm done, except that pellets kept emerging from under the seats for years.

During the nineteen years I raced my 3-wheel Morgan, I had an octagonal MG badge affixed with putty over the Morgan radiator badge. This elicited many comments, like, "I didn't know MG built three-wheel cars."

My answer was, "According to MG history, in 1934 there was a shortage of wheels due to backorders, so the factory produced 18 three-wheel cars, and this is one of them." This new fable appeared, with pictures, in several publications.

The following article was written by my friend, Peter Darnall, and was published in the December 2004 issue of *Victory Lane* magazine. The pictures of the MG badge and me were included in the article. (Peter stretched the facts a wee bit, but it's still pretty funny!)

"Have you heard any good Morgan stories lately?
What about the legend of the MG Morgan? Was there some sort of association between the Morgan Motor Company and the MG Car Company that produced a limited number of 3-wheelers in the mid 1930's? Like most undocumented car stories, this one is probably poppycock and should not be taken seriously.

"But, then again, it just might have been true.

"I came across this story in a video on Speed Channel TV some time ago. I vaguely remember the commentator, possibly Alan DeCadenet, telling a story about a rare MG Morgan. It seemed that the founder of the Morgan Company, H.F.S. Morgan, had encountered some financial difficulties in the early 1930's and was seeking monetary assistance. The banks were in the midst of the Depression and weren't willing to provide the money. He turned to his friend and competitor Cecil Kimber. Cecil Kimber was the founder of the MG Car Company. Kimber agreed to provide the funding Morgan needed with the stipulation that the cars produced under this arrangement would carry an MG octagon badge. There were, perhaps, 14 three-wheel cars produced that carried the MG badge.

"I was never able to find anybody that knew anything about the MG Morgans until this year at the Monterey Historics. I had come across my friend, Al Moss, in the paddock. Al was running his 1934 Morgan SS "trike" in the pre-war sports and touring car group. Al Moss knows his cars very well and has been involved with the sports car movement on the West Coast from the very early days following World War II. He had been the Los Angeles area dealer for Allard Motor Cars. His company, Moss Motors, was a leading mail order supplier of parts for British sports cars for many years. He had restored the Morgan himself and took real pride in the authenticity of the car.

"Al Moss is also well known for his mischievous sense of humor. One intuitively checks for a hidden whoopee cushion before sitting down in any chair offered by Al. The stories of his pranks are very much an integral part of sports car scene in

Southern California. When I saw the MG octagon badge on the radiator shell of his Morgan, I should have been forewarned that things were not as they should have been. His evasive answer to my question about the MG badge dodged the issue.

"The original Morgan emblem was damaged and I wanted something to temporarily cover the spot. I had an old MG octagonal badge lying around and it was a perfect fit."

"That explained how the MG badge came to be mounted on Al's Morgan. It did not explain how the legend of the MG Morgans came to be or how a documentary video could have been created which made actual reference to these cars. After some prodding, Al revealed the rest of the story. His face turned red, almost the same color as his driving suit, as he recalled that embarrassing moment. One of his "little jokes" had gotten out of hand.

"It happened a few years ago at a previous Monterey Historics event, Al looked up to see a documentary film crew descending on his Morgan in the paddock area. Eventually someone in the group noticed the MG badge and asked him about it. Rather than admit that he had used the MG badge to cover a hole, he came up with the cock-and-bull story of Cecil Kimber and the MG Morgans on the spur of the moment. He even claimed that his Morgan was the last of 14 cars produced that carried the MG badge and that it was the only one known to exist today. At this moment, unable to contain his laughter any longer, he dived under the rear deck lid of the Morgan and pretended to make some mechanical adjustment. After a long moment, he regained his composure and prepared to tell the film crew about his little joke with them.

"To his dismay, the film crew had left and were nowhere in sight. He looked around the paddock, but they had apparently packed up and gone for the day. He claimed that he had no idea that the cameras were running or that his story had been recorded. Al Moss' tall tale of the MG Morgan eventually became part of a video and the legend of the MG Morgan was born."

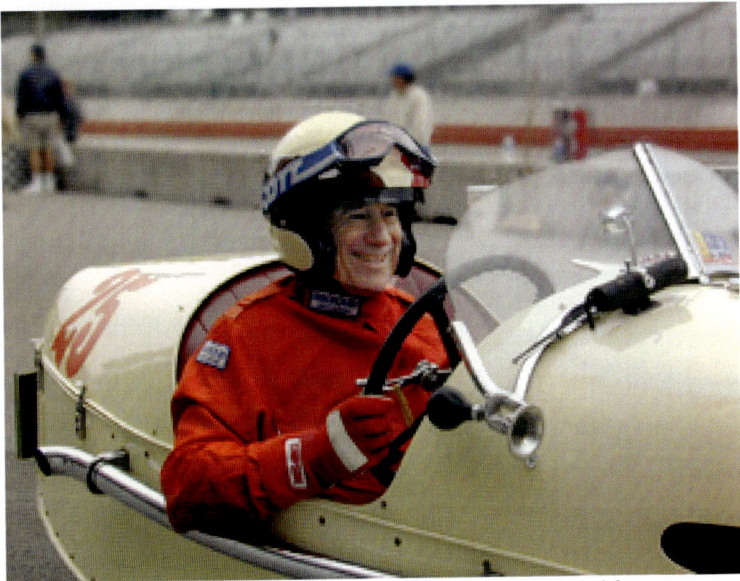

These photos, taken by Peter Darnall, were used in his article.

In 1953 I turned this little girl loose at a Concours with a realistic-looking, hollow rubber hammer. It couldn't hurt anything, but it sure scared a lot of exhibitors!

It's hell, getting old.

29 Cars I Have Owned

In addition to the various cars I have described in previous chapters, I will describe a few of the other interesting cars I've owned.

By far the most interesting and exotic of my cars was the 1938 Talbot Lago coupe with a Figoni & Falaschi "teardrop" body. Twelve similar cars were made, three of which came to New York, and were purchased by Tommy Lee, a wealthy sportsman from Los Angeles, who added them to his stable. Upon his death, the collection was dispersed and John von Neumann purchased one of the Talbots. I saw this very car in 1948 and fell in love with it. I purchased the car in 1952 for $2850, cherished and drove it for nine months, and sold it for $3300 – a *great* profit on a car worth millions today.

It was a fantastic car to drive and, naturally, attracted attention wherever it went.

I took this photo at the Davis track in 1948, when John von Neumann owned the car. It is being driven here by Fred (Bill) Proctor.

The Talbot was red when I owned it.

A far cry from cars like the Talbot, were several American Bantam cars I owned: two roadsters, a sedan and a rare pickup truck. These cars were based on the English Austin and were a true, small automobile. They could be driven anywhere, especially if one was not in a hurry to get there.

Many Bantams were featured in pranks – like ending up in college hallways. Spike Jones band member, Doodles Weaver, once drove his Austin-Bantam down the main hall of Los Angeles High School.

I was also the proud owner, briefly, of a Mk IV Jaguar convertible, a MK V Jaguar sedan and a "coffin-nose" Cord 810 cabriolet. And a favorite was one of two Jaguar XK-120 roadsters that I owned, at the same time. They were sleek, quiet, fast and enjoyable to drive.

Of course, my all-time favorite has to be the MG TC, which I purchased new, and still drive and race regularly.

The TC

1931 Chevy

1940 Bantam

1950 Sunbeam Talbot

1950 J-2 Cadillac Allard

1941 Willys Americar

1966 Simca Aronde

1947 Cadillac, before…

…and after

1948 Jaguar Mk IV

1950 Jaguar Mk V

1967 Mustang 390

1936 Cord Cabriolet (like mine)

1987 Honda CRX Si

1976 Jaguar XJ-12C (coupe)

1990 Nissan 300 ZX

1931 Packard (1/2 mine)

1949 MG Y-Type, before…

… and after

1956 LeMans Healey 100, before…

…and after

161

1968 MGB before…

…and after my restoration.

London Beardmore taxi c1956

2006 Miata SuperSport

My 2 XK-120 Jaguars, a 1951 and a 1953

1924 Bugatti Type 35. Not mine, but I maintain and drive it.

30   **Backward**

All books begin with a foreword. Well, mine ends with a ~~backward~~ backword.

I turned 80 at the beginning of 2007, and two fantastic surprise parties celebrated the great occasion. The first was at a Santa Barbara restaurant, shortly before my birthday. It was organized by my longtime friend, companion, helper and cohort, Lynda McEvoy, assisted by my daughter, Juli. More than 70 of my good friends from both the car and horse worlds were invited. Was I ever shocked when the doors to the back room opened and the invited guests shouted "Surprise."

Then, on the night of my birthday, our good friend, Ellie Haga hosted the second party in Sedona – a catered dinner at her house. That night, as our car approached Ellie's house after dark, I was totally surprised to see the street filled with people waving checkered flags.

So, now that I am an octogenarian, at the urging of both of my friends, I decided to write an autobiography – a book largely about myself and autos – isn't that what an auto-biography is supposed to be – a book about autos? I truly hope you enjoy reading it as much as I did writing it.

Finally, I wish to express my deep and sincere appreciation to the following friends who assisted, in so many ways, with the preparation of this book: Peter Egan, Richie Mayer, Lynda McEvoy, Ed Pittman, Maxi Riggs and Lon Walters. Thank you all for taking the time to edit my manuscript.

Remember, it's never too late to have a happy childhood.

Happy Motoring,

Al Moss

My, what a handsome devil I am!

Lynda's not too bad looking, either!